# SOCIETY, SCHOOLS, AND TEACHER PREPARATION:
## A Report of the Commission on the Future Education of Teachers

## Association of Teacher Educators

Donald E. Orlosky
Editor

Published by

Association of Teacher Educators
and

LB
1715
.S63
1988

American Association of Colleges for Teacher Education
One Dupont Circle, NW, Suite 610, Washington, DC
20036

May 1988

CITE AS:
Orlosky, Donald E. (Ed.) (1988). Society, Schools, and Teacher Preparation. A Report of the Commission on the Future Education of Teachers (Teacher Education Monograph No. 9). Washington, DC: ERIC Clearinghouse on Teacher Education.


MANUSCRIPTS:
The ERIC Clearinghouse on Teacher Education invites individuals to submit proposals for writing monographs for the Teacher Education Monograph Series. Proposals should include:

1. A detailed manuscript proposal of not more than five pages.
2. A vita.
3. A writing sample.


ORDERS:
ERIC CLEARINGHOUSE ON TEACHER EDUCATION
One Dupont Circle, NW, Suite 610
Washington, DC 20036
(202) 293-2450


Library of Congress Catalog Card Number: 88-080932

ISBN 0-89333-050-7


Series Editor: Mary E. Dilworth
Technical Editor: Barbara Baron

**OERI**

*Office of Educational*
*Research and Improvement*
*U.S. Department of Education*

This publication was prepared with funding from the Office of Educational Research and Improvement, U.S. Department of Education under contract number 400-86-0033. The opinions expressed in this report do not necessarily reflect the positions or policies of OERI or DOE.

# Contents

# Contributors

**Joel L. Burdin**
Professor of Educational Administration
City University of New York

**William Georgiades**
Dean, College of Education
University of Houston

**Joan Inglis**
Professor of Education
University of Toledo

**Howard Mehlinger**
Dean, School of Education
University of Indiana

**Donald E. Orlosky**
Chairman, Department of Educational Leadership
University of South Florida

**Chris Pipho**
Director, Information Clearinghouse
Education Commission of the States

# Preface

The Commission on the Future Education of Teachers was appointed in 1985 to make recommendations concerning the future preparation of teachers. At the time of its appointment, published reports had already circulated suggesting ways that schools might be upgraded, teacher education improved, and the nation's economy strengthened through education. Many of these reports focused on improving conditions in schools, creating teacher incentives, establishing new patterns for pre-service preparation, and developing new career patterns for professional teachers. All these recommendations are now in the process of being considered and, to a limited degree, implemented.

The previous reports tend to have similar goals pertaining to school reform, but often differ on the best way to achieve them. Some regard increased funding as critical in creating a better system of incentives in order to solve the dual problem of teacher shortage and teacher quality. Others recommend a change in structure, viz., that aspiring teachers should receive professional education in graduate school as doctors, lawyers and other professionals do. (The disadvantage of this approach is that it would limit teacher education institutions to those able to meet certain standards regarding faculty and facilities for research, instruction and field experience, and would eliminate many competent teachers and undergraduate programs that are currently needed to meet the demand for new teachers. This approach appeals to those for whom the elevation of professional standards and prestige represents the best way to attract more qualified candidates and improve public regard for teachers.) Most of the reports also address the differences between fifth year programs that follow an undergraduate degree, five-year programs that combine teacher preparation with a degree, and traditional four-year programs, either directly or by implication. The proliferation of reports and diverse recommendations in the field make it clear that the task of preparing sufficient numbers of qualified, talented teachers is a monumental undertaking.

Institutions interested in reform must decide whether to overhaul their programs, continue present practices, make slight modifications, or eliminate teacher preparation programs altogether. This report takes the position that careful modification rather than comprehensive revision will enable the teaching profession to deal with problems without incurring such risks as the loss of prospective teachers or undermining institutions already making an essential contribution to teaching. On the other hand, this Commission applauds those institutions with the psychological climate, resources, and leadership that make it feasible for them to completely revise their courses, create innovative programs, and develop new and effective ways to prepare teachers. However, the forthcoming teacher shortage, combined with uncertainties as to the best way to train new professionals makes it wise, in the eyes of this Commission, to retain several options in the kinds of preparation programs offered.

This Commission wishes to credit its members, whose qualifications and background were a major strength in writing this report. All the members—professors, department chairs, deans, and supervisors of student teaching—have had extensive public school experience and a long history of working with teacher education programs. In addition, they have often worked with teachers and other school officials on school concerns, including professional preparation. Their combined production in research, writing, participation in professional organizations, and involvement in major movements has been continuous over the last several decades. Their experience, knowledge, and values, accumulated during career-long immersion in the issues contained in this report, provide some of the "documentation" underlying its recommendations and narrative.

The members of the Commission contributed considerable time and energy to this task. Their work was completed without financial support from any organization or foundation, requiring them to support themselves through personal or institutional resources. The work was accomplished through periodic meetings and shared writing tasks, with review taking place by correspondence.

This report is divided into sections; each topic was personally selected and written by a Commission member, with the result that there are stylistic differences throughout. The sections and their authors are: "The New America for the Third Millenium," by William Georgiades; "Teacher Supply and Demand," by Chris Pipho; "Technology and Teaching," by Howard Mehlinger; "Governance Issues in the Education Profession," by Joan Inglis; "Schools, Communities, and the Private Sector," by Joel L. Burdin. The remaining sections—including the Preface, Introduction, and Epilogue—were written by Donald E. Orlosky, Commission chairman. W. Robert Houston, former president of the Association of Teacher Educators, appointed this Commission and reviewed the manuscript. Kenneth Howey served on this body and contributed to the research used in the final report. The ATE Communications Committee also reviewed a draft of the report and provided valuable suggestions.

Although many individuals helped in reviewing or making other substantial contributions to this document, the chairman assumes ultimate responsibility for the final version, which may not necessarily reflect the views of all contributors. This report does not necessarily reflect the position of ATE on the issues addressed. Nevertheless, the support and encouragement of those who helped prepare this document, the initial stimulus from ATE, and the cooperation of the ERIC Clearinghouse on Teacher Education in facilitating production are deeply appreciated.

Donald E. Orlosky
Chairman

# Introduction

About every 20 years, a "crisis" develops in education, with the public and teaching profession bombarded with recommendations on how to make schools more effective. Today, we are again barraged with reports on how to improve schools. Such reports often goad legislators into passing regulations and requirements which, though well-intended, do not improve schools, but instead complicate the already difficult job of teaching. Genuine improvement depends on quality instruction, which cannot be provided without competent teachers; on first-rate facilities, materials, and equipment; and on a supportive organizational structure. Teachers need to be relieved of the excessive demands of clerical, administrative, and supervisory work for which little or no time is allotted them. Schools are most likely to be given this support by their legislatures and communities when school performance is exemplary. And, invariably, student performance is tied to teacher performance.

There is an inevitable relationship between public perception of how well the schools are doing their job and the support and resources they receive. Teachers and the work they do must be highly respected before education will be given a high priority by decision-makers. In order to perform successfully and gain this respect for teachers, schools need substantial support and a cadre of competent teachers. This is a "chicken or egg" situation. Those who feel that schools have not proven their ability to perform well may argue that an investment in schools is risky business. But denial of adequate support is not risky at all. In fact, it is a "sure thing" that most of those who grow from childhood to adulthood without obtaining the knowledge to participate in society will eventually drain the resources of the nation far beyond the cost to properly educate them in the first place. The nation can respond responsibly to educational needs today or pay more heavily tomorrow. The view in this report is that a special effort now is vital in order to avoid the crises looming ahead. Critical problems are emerging with regard to a pervasive teacher shortage, competition with other enterprises for the most able people, ethnic and racial imbalances in the teaching profession, and a lagging response in education to developments in technology, business and industry.

Thus, the major thrust of this report is to recommend procedures for the preparation of teachers. Preparation programs must be geared to the way schools operate and be flexible enough to change as schools change. This will require not so much financial support, though that is desirable,

1

as the employment of multiple resources such as different time-utilization, organizational improvement, and re-direction of existing procedures.

Teacher education has a long history that includes many successful practices that can serve as a basis for effective reform. Therefore, many familiar ideas will be found in the recommendations that follow, for certain traditional approaches deserve continuation alongside innovative ones.

Recommendations for the future preparation of teachers should include a realistic plan for excellence that reflects a concern for attracting a fair share of the "best and brightest" to the profession. Few would argue with this premise, but views differ on the best way to achieve it. Despite considerable progress in determining the characteristics of effective teachers, the data are incomplete. In addition, important aspects of teaching are idiosyncratic and the characteristics and competencies of effective teachers diverse. Therefore, reports on teacher preparation are necessarily somewhat subjective and reflect the experiences of those who write them. This report is no exception. The following statements are provided as a transition and orientation to the premises on which the recommendations presented throughout this paper are based.

1. An effective teacher is central to school success and one of the best bargains the American public has ever had. The creation of schools in which one adult and a classroomful of youth come together to meet the educational requirements of a nation is a monumental task. (The inherent complexity of schools, with all the diversity of personalities, social interactions, and intellectual expectations presents a set of variables whose combinations and permutations are beyond calculation. It is a minor miracle that schools work well at all; in fact, it can be said they work amazingly well.)

Anyone who has observed the efforts conscientious teachers apply to their students must be impressed with the energy, dedication and skill the public reaps for its investment in education. The public must understand, however, that future recruitment of such dedicated professionals will depend on incentives that are needed a) to attract a competitive share of the most qualified and talented teachers available, and b) to strengthen the ranks of the profession for the tough challenges ahead.

2. Public schools are incredibly complex institutions that enroll students from a wide spectrum of socio-economic, ethnic, racial, and religious populations. Pupils may come from homes that have loving, abusive, or neglectful parents; from high, low, or middle socio-economic conditions; and from communities with attitudes that range from full support to open hostility towards school. They also have emotional and

intellectual differences that are further complicated by their interests, varied energy, and capacity to learn. The needs these different circumstances create make it difficult to determine the "proper" role of schools vis-a-vis that which belongs to society.

If schools claim to provide optimal learning for all students, to remedy social ills, and establish high standards for each new generation, they will inevitably over-promise and under-deliver, leaving the nation frustrated by the inadequacy of high school graduates. It is clear schools cannot be held solely responsible for the "products" that emerge from today's classrooms. (No industry would advertise zero-defects if it had no control over the quality of its raw material.) Society must also do its part, which is not limited to footing the bill, setting goals, and demanding high standards. Social institutions such as the family, social agencies, businesses, industries, churches, recreational programs, and other enterprises all must contribute towards the successful transition of youth into adulthood. Successful reform is only possible, however, if the separate, interdependent roles of society and schools are realistically clarified.

3. The fundamental responsibility of schools is the reduction of ignorance through systematic transmission of knowledge. If the schools fail to provide students with the opportunity to acquire knowledge, no other institution can replace this deficiency. However, this goal must be achieved and modified within the context of a highly diverse student population. High standards, for example, are vital but they must not be so rigidly applied that students with weak academic potential are driven prematurely from schools into a society that has no place for them. In such cases, the professional knowledge of the competent teacher who understands rates of maturing, stages of development, and the consequences of destructive pressure in the "learn at all cost" climate sometimes created by an overzealous public, must be respected.

4. Realistic measures are more likely than utopian ones to be implemented in improving schools and teacher preparation programs. Dramatic recommendations attract headlines and are often embraced by those who live in the world of hope instead of reality. There is much to commend in those who dream, including the members of this Commission who sometimes wish for such total change as the tripling of salaries, drastic reduction of teacher work loads, and such high professional status that only the most outstanding members of each new generation would be chosen to teach. However, it is no service to the profession to ask for unrealistic reform when the necessary resources and philosophical support are lacking.

5. Pedagogical learning is an essential part of teacher education programs. A successful teacher must be competent not only in subject content and general knowledge, but must also have pedagogical knowl-

edge and skills. Criticisms of teacher preparation sometimes focus on the alleged dominance of pedagogy in preparation programs which, purportedly, leave insufficient time for academic study, and produce teachers who are academically deficient. Teachers need more than academic preparation alone, however. Good classroom teaching depends on knowledge of research in educational effectiveness, on proper diagnosis of learning needs, and on delivery of instruction that is appropriate to those needs. A suitable academic background, high intelligence, and good will are not enough. Teacher preparation must include training in pedagogical skills, along with the acquisition of specialized and general academic knowledge. All of these are essential components of teacher preparation.

In brief, the improvements needed in schools are based on the premises that 1) effective teachers are essential for successful schools, 2) schools are complex institutions that require help from the community, 3) schools are uniquely responsible for the systematic transmission of knowledge, 4) recommendations that are feasible and realistic are most likely to be implemented, and 5) both pedagogical and academic preparation are essential for teacher preparation. These premises form a backdrop for the discussions and recommendations developed by this Commission.

The following background material provides salient features of the development of education in this country. It is important to recognize the value of previous events that explain present circumstances and provide sound principles on which to base future changes. It is also mandatory to observe the journal of negative findings developed from past experience in order to avoid repeating the mistakes of our predecessors.

## BACKGROUND

School reform is slow and complex, requiring time and patience as well as energy, resources, and ideas to be successful. (This is fortuitous, for hasty change, while expedient at the time, is incompatible with the realities of legitimate change, is disruptive, and fosters more discord than harmony.)

The topic of reform has been a subject of concern in this nation for the past century or more. However, it is appropriate to begin here with the 1888 speech by Charles W. Eliot, then president of Harvard, when he asked if school programs could be shortened and improved. His complaint that students began school too late and remained too long led to the establishment of the 1893 report of the Committee of Ten. Their report recommended a lock-step curriculum, rigorous standards, and reduction of grammar and secondary school from twelve to eleven years. In the midst of these traditional and conservative views, Joseph Rice, who had

4

visited Europe to examine the European approach to education, reflected the views of Rousseau and Pestalozzi in his articles in the *Forum* which proposed a more tolerant attitude towards the interests of youth in planning schools. These two approaches could be translated roughly into progressive and traditional views which formed the poles of a continuum that followed well into the present century.

On the heels of the Committee of Ten report and concurrently with the implications of their recommendations, a series of events transpired that consumed the efforts of educators for at least six or seven more decades. Binet and Simon in France developed the intelligence test which was eventually translated by Terman into English. Edward L. Thorndike began the study of learning around the turn of the century, continuing his exceptionally productive work into the 1930's. His theories and research included the Law of Readiness, Law of Practice, and Law of Effect, which focused on scientific inquiry into the process of learning in regard to practice, disuse, reward, dissatisfaction, forgetting, and retention. John Dewey influenced educators by his writing and teaching about the merits of progressivism and social reconstruction through schooling. School leaders began to look at reorganization possibilities and—among other innovations—opened the first junior high school doors in 1909.

The social unrest of the first two decades of this century saw the emergence of social programs, influenced in part by Jacob Riis' writings, *Children of the Poor* and *How the Other Half Lives.* The mental health movement also received a boost from Clifford Beers work, *A Mind that Found Itself,* a personal story of a cured psychotic. The sweat shops of the industrial areas, the lack of compulsory school attendance, the women's suffrage issue, and the abuses found in city tenement living awakened the nation's social conscience and created a climate for the establishment of the American Civil Liberties Union (1916), special programs such as Jane Addams's Hull House in Chicago, and the passage of the 19th Amendment granting women the right to vote (1920).

Thus, the conservatism of the 1880's, the psychological inquiry and ideological differences of the 1900's, and the establishment of laws and organizations in the 1920's provide a sketch of social and school events that created some of the major social themes to which schools responded. Some of these responses included:

1. Compulsory attendance laws.
2. Methods courses that taught the new psychology in teaching.
3. The opening of junior high schools designed to adapt education to the adolescent age.
4. The formation of philosophical issues, which led to debates over the school curriculum.
5. The development of concern for the "whole child," including

intellectual and personal development.

6. The development of the idea that school programs should come from society and return to enrich it, i.e., school programs should respond to the needs of society.

By the 1940's, the nation's schools had undergone a period of trial and error, experimentation, reorganization, and criticism and analysis against a backdrop of the prohibition and speakeasies era of the 1920's and the great depression of the 1930's. This twenty year period saw the formation of the Progressive Education Association (1919); The Eight Year Study (1933-1941) that assessed the effect of experimental and traditional high school curricula on college success; the continual examination of social reconstruction through the writings of George Count's well-known pamphlet, *Dare the Schools Build a New Social Order?* (1932); and the beginning of *Life Adjustment Education,* as proposed by Charles Prosser. During this time, John Dewey continued promoting his progressive views, while conservative opposition was expressed by C.W. Bagley, Henry Morrison, W.W. Charters and, at times, Elwood C. Cubberly. Thorndike continued his experimental work and published a major revision of his findings during the 1930's. Sidney Pressey initiated the basic ideas behind teaching machines (programmed instruction) using evidence from Thorndike, but a lack of resources and computers doomed another idea before its time.

The stage was set for another round of debate and controversy when the attack on Pearl Harbor in 1941 and U.S. entry into World War II channeled the nation's energy into fighting its enemies. The end of the war in 1945 ushered in a time of celebration and a return to the routines of peacetime living. This was soon disrupted in the early 1950's by the rise of various intense and persistent educational issues that filled the literature of the day. Admiral Rickover proposed such changes as science education and mathematics for the gifted, to improve U.S. competitiveness worldwide. Arthur Bestor, head of the Council for Basic Education, and history professor at Illinois University, wrote *Educational Wastelands* and *Restoration of Learning.* Rudolph Flesch described why Johnny can't read in a book of the same title. The critics of life-adjustment education wrote about *Lollipops vs. Learning* and all the issues we are familiar with regarding censorship, evolution, sex-education, religion, values, segregation, and Communism as a threat to democracy. The critical media spared no one—including teachers, administrators, textbooks, and school standards in their attacks. The launching of the Soviet space ship, Sputnik, in 1957 seemed to give the charges credibility, and when the humanists responded with the Association for Supervision and Curriculum Development (ASCD) publication, *Becoming, Behaving, Perceiving* (1962), the time was ripe for another showdown in education.

However, as the 1960's issues emerged, educators raised new questions themselves, and reacted to criticism differently than before. Past experience had shown that winning arguments by shouting louder and longer than the critics only silenced them temporarily, but did not solve inherent problems, which soon returned. The profession, with support from federal resources, started to examine the knowledge base on which teaching was founded. The research of Thorndike began to make more of an impact than the views of Dewey. A series of educational research and development laboratories launched investigations to augment the sparse scientific findings of individual educational researchers with more systematic, long-range, and substantial results to determine the "truth" about what makes schools work effectively.

The early 1970's bore witness to an embarrassing admission by the profession that a substantial research base for teaching, teacher certification, and teacher preparation was lacking. Substantive answers were hard to find to questions that critics of the sixties raised in such books as *The Mis-Education of American Teachers,* by Koerner; *The Education of American Teachers,* by Conant; and *The Great Training Robbery,* by Greer. The debate on teacher education was given new direction by issues of accountability, the early research on teaching through micro-teaching, interaction analysis, protocol materials, mini-course and modules on teacher performance, and the establishment of Competence Based Teacher Education.

The early 1980's saw a new wave of recommendations for reform in such reports as *A Nation at Risk, The Paedia Proposal, Horace's Compromise,* and *High School.* Again, the nation's frustration with school performance became a media issue. The situation was mollified, however, by important new developments. First, the profession had matured and was utilizing current knowledge to wrestle with some of its own problems, applying scientific inquiry to the accepted conventional wisdom of the past. Secondly, the tone of the critics' reform recommendations seemed more positive, reinforced by a spirit of cooperation and support. The reformers were more benign and eager to build on the strengths of the schools. A third factor was the realization that much more was at stake, requiring that the necessary cooperation be marshalled to set a positive course of action for education.

As the dust settled from the reports of the early eighties, there were several new developments in the field. Two important groups issued reports on teacher preparation: *Preparing Tomorrow's Teachers,* by the Holmes Group; and *A Nation Prepared: Teachers for the 21st Century,* by the Carnegie Forum on Education and the Economy. The National Council for Accreditation of Teacher Education prepared a redesign of teaching standards. And the Blue Ribbon Task Force of the Association of Teacher Educators prepared an analysis of the three reports.

The time now seems especially urgent, and conditions ripe, for using the ideas of the present and the lessons of the past to build a future ready to cope with the crucial issues of society and schools. The remainder of this report presents recommendations for improving teacher preparation programs, followed by a number of themes that develop their underlying rationale. The themes, selected on the basis of their significance, are: 1) Fundamental Reforms, 2) The New America for the Third Millenium (Demographic Trends and Consequences), 3) Teacher Supply and Demand, 4) Technology and Teaching, 5) Governance, and 6) Relationships with the Community.

# I

## Fundamental Reforms

An old riddle asks, "If you call a dog's tail a leg, how many legs does it have?" The answer to the riddle is that the dog still has four legs. Calling a tail a leg doesn't make it one. Saying the schools need a major overhaul doesn't necessarily make it so. It is evident that the mechanisms required to manage the huge enterprise called public education have evolved over a long period of time into an organization that makes schooling available to everyone. The fact that it works imperfectly obligates the nation to seek improvements. The fact that it works as well as it does suggests modifying rather than razing the structure.

This can be done by working with four basic areas that lend themselves to fundamental and manageable reforms, and can provide the foundation for improving education across the country, i.e., personnel, governance, incentives, and pedagogy.

### PERSONNEL

Reforms in the area of personnel have to deal with the projected teacher shortage, which this Commission has found to be real and multi-faceted. The dimensions of the problem include an uneven supply of teachers in various academic areas, as well as shortages in different geographical regions, socio-economic settings, and racial and ethnic representation. Those who would question the lack of teachers in these categories must surely acknowledge the "brain drain" that draws prospective teachers to other fields of work where incentives and conditions are more attractive.

Some claim the teacher shortage can be solved by raising standards and increasing professional status. The assumption that elevating "standards" to an impressively high level will attract more, not fewer well-qualified people to the profession is clearly a gamble. If it paid off, teaching performance throughout the profession would probably reach an all-time high. If it failed, the result would be that schools would have fewer competent teachers, with supplementary recruits from alternative certification programs who would likely be marginally prepared teachers and/or a large number of aides, para-professionals, and volunteers.

This Commission supports higher standards and strongly endorses the importance of elevating selection and preparation programs to the highest possible level. But the question remains "What constitutes higher standards?" Some recommend five-year programs with the first four years devoted mainly to liberal arts, followed by screening criteria for admission into a professional pedagogical program. This is a risky proposition that would delay preparation for teaching and remove pedagogy from the current four-year programs. No one can be certain about the consequences of such a change, but the following drawbacks seem likely.

Undergraduate students who have developed a sense of momentum toward the teaching profession might lose their energy and interest if their training were delayed until a fifth year. Of course, there is no assurance their interest would wane, but teacher preparation educators who note the enthusiasm and eagerness in such undergraduates consider it a definite asset to their training and motivation.

The number of institutions that prepare teachers would be drastically reduced. (Of course, those that offer subminimal preparation should not continue, but the accreditation and/or state approval process is the proper vehicle for these cases.) Many of the casualties would include four-year liberal arts colleges that currently attract some of the nation's best high school students. Other casualties would include highly qualified faculty and students who constitute an important professional resource. Undergraduate programs in teacher education would also be adversely affected by the loss of students who might chose to defer training.

The danger of instituting four-year pre-professional programs focused on liberal arts is that it could disrupt the present teacher preparation structure without improving the quality of instruction in public school classrooms. Since there is no evidence that such four-year programs will improve teaching, and since fifth year programs have not been in operation long enough to be evaluated, it is wiser to strengthen and continue the present track alongside the development of experimental programs. This Commission holds the view that both four- and five-year programs of teacher preparation can serve the nation well, for they permit diverse institutions to educate teachers, opening the profession to the widest array of capable undergraduates. The Commission recommends setting requirements that will raise the average level of entrants, attract an increasingly high number of outstanding new teachers, alter the pre-service curriculum, and retain the options of four- and five-year programs.

Another area of concern in the supply-demand issues is how to recruit more teachers from all sectors of the population. Quota systems that would employ teachers for reasons other than their competence are counter-productive in the long run and amount to social engineering. This approach not only harms such recruits and promotes negative reactions from the public, but also damages the reputation of the many competent minority teachers in the profession. There are other positive inducements that should be used to attract minorities without waiving admission or completion requirements, i.e., scholarship and loan programs, and other benefits based on merit. It is important for minority recruitment to succeed, in order that future generations of minority students, aspiring teachers, and other segments of the population have appropriate role models. A united effort is necessary to achieve this, requiring all sectors of society—school guidance departments, families, communities, business, and government and social agencies—to help find promising minority teachers.

A third area of importance is the need to obtain teachers willing and able to teach in content areas where there are shortages. The preferred solution to this problem is, again, incentives that will attract capable people to all areas of teaching. It is important not to show favoritism towards those teaching in areas of short supply, to avoid problems of low morale and dissension among teachers of other areas. A later discussion will deal with this issue and make recommendations on how this might be accomplished.

One of the major concerns of teacher recruitment is the problem of attracting teachers to schools with severe problems, where the students drop out in large numbers (more than 50 percent in some cases), vandalize school property, engage in seriously disruptive and destructive behavior, have many pregnancies, and easily become addicted to alcohol and drugs.

The problem here is much bigger than the schools alone can solve. Society must form partnerships with a variety of agencies to address these problems by studying programs with good records, and establishing and implementing experimental programs on a trial basis. After sufficient knowledge has accumulated concerning the best way to cope with such problems (assuming it is possible to do so), these programs should be replicated throughout the nation. An emergency task force should then be established to design programs and determine the resources needed to reform schools with the greatest problems. At the same time, teacher preparation and inservice programs must be established to identify the best qualified teachers who are willing to make a significant difference in these problem schools and in the students and communities concerned.

One final areas for discussion is the use of para-professionals and teacher aides to alleviate part of the supply-demand problem. Considerable success with volunteers and aides is evident in many school districts which capitalize on the talents and energies of other adults in the community, particularly young retirees. Many of these people have much to offer in the way of special talents, knowledge, or skills, and can be employed to help in vocational areas; areas of content, particularly basic subjects such as reading and mathematics; or with clerical or supervisory tasks.

Other areas of support include businesses that "adopt-a-school," supplying experts who donate instruction and expertise to students, and support groups that raise funds and other resources for schools. Care must be taken, however, to recruit suitable people, utilizing screening and selective criteria, to ensure that both schools and volunteers are served well.

People untrained in pedagogy can be helpful to the schools if they receive instruction and supervision in their given tasks. Each school must make certain that volunteers understand its particular philosophy toward students; understand their own limits in dealing with students; and possess (or can easily acquire) the knowledge they need to provide helpful service. Despite a certain amount of risk inherent in such ventures, the potential value of volunteers and employed aides is too high to overlook as a resource for education.

To encapsulate, the supply-demand issue should be addressed by 1) continuing to obtain teachers through four-year and five-year programs, 2) launching even greater efforts to attract the most able minorities, 3) providing incentives that will attract teachers across all grade levels and academic areas, 4) creating special incentives and support to encourage teachers to serve in the nation's most difficult schools, and 5) recruiting capable para-professionals, volunteers, aides and qualified people from business, industry and other community resources. It should not be overlooked, however, that the most fundamental change needed to cope with problems of teacher quality and supply is improved employment conditions and financial incentives for teachers.

## GOVERNANCE

A nother important factor that encourages or discourages prospective teachers is the element of teacher control over the profession. The critical factors involved include certification requirements, professional practices and ethics, and participation at the local and state level in establishing policy and procedures. State legislatures and local boards presently determine and enforce policies in these areas. However, professional educators must become the dominant force in setting standards for licensure and acceptable professional behavior. To do this, they must be willing to set their own standards and police their own ranks. If they are to create a full-fledged profession, they must form a united front of teachers, supervisors, principals, and teacher education professors.

These groups are charged with the responsibility to make schools and teaching conditions as good as possible; however, they are often viewed as separate parts of the profession. This artificial splintering into sub-groups creates false barriers and an impression that they lack common goals, or may even be working at cross-purposes. A cooperative arrangement must be established among them, and those with essential responsibility in teacher preparation must be given a role in governing the profession.

## INCENTIVES

Incentives come in several forms and their appeal depends on their timing in a teacher's career. The beginning teacher may select a position on the basis of location. The experienced teacher may remain in the profession if recognition and working conditions are satisfying. Another may be attracted to a particular kind of assignment and yet another may find that motivated pupils perpetuate an interest in teaching. But the one common element that can attract and keep good teachers is a salary structure that provides a decent standard of living and rewards the best teachers for their excellence.

The teachers of this nation should be able to marry and enjoy a standard of living commensurate with their professional preparation and responsibility. Beginning teachers should be paid a salary competitive with starting salaries for other college graduates entering engineering, business, marketing, or managerial positions. They should not be forced to make a choice between teaching and a reasonable standard of living.

It is a relatively simple matter to prescribe that beginning teachers should earn more money (perhaps $25,000-$30,000 in today's economy) and increase their earnings as they gain experience towards a maximum wage level ($60,000-$75,000). This prescription, however, generates positive responses from educators and the classic arguments from society that reflect the fundamental belief that "any profession that pays its very best and its very worst the same can't expect to receive strong support or high status." It is clear, therefore, that some procedures need to be installed to provide differential pay acceptable to the public and the profession. Merit pay plans have fallen short and created morale problems. Other alternatives are possible and should be launched on a pilot basis. (Only a sketchy outline of some of these is described in this report as the details require thorough analysis and careful planning to avoid serious errors.)

One recommended approach is for school districts to identify crucial tasks that require additional time and energy but must be done. These include curriculum development; textbook reviews; selection of instructional materials; preview and selection of software; analysis of school district data on demographics, achievement, trends, etc.; development of new programs such as parent education or exchange programs; articulation activities; school-community relationships; planning inservice programs; and creating induction programs. The time currently devoted to these tasks is provided through "unpaid overtime" with the result that they are seldom done adequately or simply never done because they require blocks of uninterrupted time.

The logical people to assume responsibility for these tasks are classroom teachers. Those who have special insight and competence could be designated "teacher-leaders" and given a supplement during the academic year, along with released time and employment for the summer vacation period. If the supplement were 10 percent of their normal nine-month contract, and the two summer months yielded another 22 percent, they would increase their normal nine-month salary by one-third.

By assigning teachers in this fashion, schools can complete many of their tasks, and classroom teachers will have more diverse, interesting, and rewarding career opportunities. The profession will also gain an edge in recruiting excellent teachers with strong leadership and organizational abilities.

The career option of becoming a teacher-leader should be open to all qualified teachers, regardless of grade level or subject area. However, a school should provide these assignments to teachers whose competence indicates they would be most likely to successfully accomplish them. The number of teachers enlisted to work in this special category would be a function of the willingness of teachers to accept these assignments. The plan would require additional funds; in a given school, however, if 10 to 20 percent of the teachers became teacher-leaders, the instructional budget would only increase about 5 to 8 percent.

Another approach for consideration is that of re-organizing the use of professional staff in a school. For example, if 10 teachers currently receive an average salary of $25,000 each, then the school district has purchased 10 professionals for $250,000. Should any of these 10 teachers leave the profession for retirement or other reasons, the normal practice would be to replace them with other professional teachers. School districts should instead consider replacing them with a variety of personnel to create a teaching team composed of a teacher-leader, five or six other teachers, and perhaps three or four para-professionals or aides. This combination would increase the number of adults versus students, and make it possible for differentiated assignments for the professional teachers on the team. These differentiated assignments would be

14

possible, in part, because the aides and para-professionals could, under the direction of the professional staff, carry out some of the clerical, supervisory, and monitoring activities that do not require a high degree of training but are tasks that currently consume valuable teacher time. A redistribution of financial resources should make it possible to employ aides at lower salaries and allot the difference to teachers according to their responsibilities. Thus, the previous 10 adults in the school would be re-aligned into 12 adults, improving the student-adult ratio by 20 percent, and at the same time freeing teachers to concentrate on duties utilizing their professional competence through the assignment of aides to routine school duties. As the schools face a reduction in professional staff and as society bulges with capable but idle people, especially among retirees, the opportunity to capitalize on this combination is at hand. Many schools are already improving their services by turning to these resources, but a more deliberate and increased effort in this direction could yield even higher dividends.

Another opportunity to identify and reward the most able teachers may arise in the near future when procedures have been established for determining board certified teachers. The intent behind the board certified teacher approach is to find the nation's most outstanding teachers and certify their exceptional competence through a procedure similar to that used in other professions. A significant effort has been launched in this direction and when credible procedures are implemented, school districts will be confronted with decisions about how to deploy these teachers. (The assumption in the recommendations that follow is that these teachers will be compensated beyond their normal pay schedule as a concomitant of meeting board certified standards.) Among the possibilities are several assignments that should be considered to keep these outstanding teachers in the classroom and utilize their unique abilities. One is to have board certified teachers work closely with beginning teachers to assist their transition into the profession. Another assignment might be for board certified teachers to work with marginal but experienced teachers, utilizing intensive supervision, demonstration teaching, coaching, and other proven techniques for strengthening weak teachers. Board certified teachers might be especially helpful to preservice teacher education programs at colleges and universities as advisors, adjuncts, supervisors of student teachers, guest lecturers and panelists, to mention a few possibilities. Of course, they also could fill teacher-leader positions during summer or serve as chairs of teaching teams.

There are many other approaches, of course. Those suggested in this section should be considered illustrative, not definitive. They are based on the following principles:

    1. Teachers who receive additional compensation should earn that

income through increased responsibility or by completing additional work, for example, during summertime or school vacations.

2. Excellent teachers should be able to receive higher income and pursue the major part of their careers as classroom teachers.
3. The assignment of extra duties for extra pay should provide better teachers with variety and professional enrichment. It is legitimate to pay an excellent teacher more for improving curriculum guides, for example, but not for lunchroom duty.

Higher compensation for teachers is an important incentive, but the quality of professional working conditions is equally important. Working conditions can be divided into two categories: the physical/material support and environmental/behavioral support.

In the area of physical and material support, it is vital that schools provide adequate supplies, sufficient clerical assistance, relief from mundane chores (e.g., supervision of buses) and tasks (e.g., running a copying machine), and an attractive setting for teaching. This can be obtained from several different sources, including the normal budget process, donations and volunteer help, and such inventive approaches as special fund-raisers, adopt-a-school programs, and other relationships with the community. School administrators, school boards, state departments of education, and legislative bodies must recognize and act appropriately to ensure adequate support for teaching. It is penny wise and pound foolish to do otherwise, when one considers the figures involved. A typical classroom may cost $80,000 to construct, with the salary of the teacher (including fringes) and normal classroom maintenance averaging more than $30,000 annually. If a classroom is used for 30 years, then it represents an outlay of about $1,000,000. An additional outlay of this cost for equipment, supplies, and other support would make this million dollar investment pay off. Yet, most classroom teachers are not provided even $500 a year for basic supplies and equipment. This lack of support is shortsighted and intolerable.

The second category of conditions required for teaching is environmental and behavioral support. Schools are "people-centered" and labor intensive. The population density in schools is high, with a wider range of diversity than other institutions. Some of the occupants, such as administrators, teachers, and support staff have chosen to be there. The vast majority (pupils), however, are required to attend. Their diverse attitudes toward learning and their countless value systems and social priorities create a school culture so complex as to test the most even-tempered at times.

In order that teachers may function effectively, school norms for behavior must be maintained. These norms require rational plans, support from all school personnel, the home, and community. There is too little opportunity in this brief section to elaborate on specific procedures that might be employed to promote a sane and productive work climate. However, it is evident from the available literature on successful schools that it is possible to maintain a productive and healthy school environment. This report supports the creation of such school conditions to make the profession more attractive to highly qualified people.

In brief, the factors required to improve teaching conditions include differentiated and higher salaries; diversity in assignments throughout a teaching career; adequate support in the form of supplies, materials, and aides; and a school organization supported by schools, parents, and community, so that schools can be safe and enjoyable places in which to work and learn.

The following list summarizes the ideas that have been presented thus far:

Recommendation 1. The incentives to attract and retain excellent teachers should be consistent across various grade levels and academic areas.

Recommendation 2. Within grade and subject areas, a variety of career patterns and incentives should be established to provide the most capable teachers with opportunities to utilize their special abilities and exercise leadership within the profession.

Recommendation 3. Teacher education institutions should focus their recruitment energies on students who are not only among the most capable, but also demonstrate the motivation and values necessary for a successful teaching career.

Recommendation 4. Teachers must be recruited from all segments of the population.

Recommendation 5. Regardless of racial, ethnic, social, or economic background, students enrolled in teacher education programs must meet admission criteria and show promise of future success as teachers.

Recommendation 6. Neither four- nor five-year programs should be abolished at the present time, as both are equipped to successfully prepare teachers.

Recommendation 7. Prototype programs and special task forces should be established to solve extreme problems in school districts that have exceptionally high rates of failure, vandalism, and students dropping-out.

Recommendation 8. The profession should employ teacher aides and obtain volunteer help through community assistance.

Recommendation 9. School aides and volunteers should be given training in their tasks.

Recommendation 10. The profession should assume responsibility for certification requirements, ethics in the teaching profession, and criteria for disciplining teachers.

Recommendation 11. Educators who participate on policy boards should represent all areas of education.

## FUTURE PREPARATION PROGRAMS

Tomorrow's society will be vastly different from today's; so will its schools. Teacher preparation programs today should strive to prepare teachers for tomorrow's educational environment. Projections concerning the society and schools of the future are always imperfect; however, it seems reasonable to factor certain predictable trends into the planning of preparation programs. The most relevant trends and concerns are as follows:

1. Major demographic changes will affect all teacher preparation programs and require the revision of all recruitment efforts.
2. The traditional teaching career becomes static and uninteresting over the course of a lifetime and results in the under-utilization of talented teachers as well. A variety of assignments must be infused into teaching careers, and preparation programs must be made responsive to new career configurations.
3. Distinctions should be made among preparation programs, with three different grade levels of schooling delineated: secondary school, junior high/middle school, and elementary school. School districts typically include these three levels, following the approximate pattern of grades K-5, 6-8, and 9-12.
4. Incentives must be established to attract talented students to teaching, increase the morale of experienced teachers, and improve the status of the profession.
5. Recruitment and selection procedures must make certain that teacher education candidates have the academic interest, ability, and desire to teach. Recruitment and selection will be facilitated when a combination of criteria, incentives, and challenging preparation programs exists to draw more qualified candidates to the field.
6. Teacher preparation programs must utilize the knowledge gained through research and experience in order to make schools and teachers more effective.
7. Prospective teachers should have access to technological training in order to increase their effectiveness.
8. The preservice program must have a balanced curriculum of liberal arts, content specialization, and pedagogical preparation to equip teacher candidates for challenging professional careers.

Based on these considerations, this Commission recommends that teacher preparation programs contain the five elements of basic studies, content specialization, content methodology, pedagogy, and laboratory and field-based programs.

The purpose of the basic studies component is to ensure that all teachers are introduced to the following areas of study: social studies, science, humanities, psychology and physical health. This component would extend the liberal arts background of education students, help them to explore their own individual interests, and broaden their intellectual background. It would also help them identify an area of specialization; help them become conversant in many areas; promote further development (formally or informally) by stimulating their intellectual curiosity; and integrate areas of knowledge through their understanding of the similarities and differences of various disciplines.

Typically, students would focus their entire first year in basic studies, which would be identical to that taken by undergraduates bound for other professions. In total, the basic studies component would cover about one-third of the preservice undergraduate program.

The content specialization area should vary according to the level a prospective teacher plans to teach and should occupy about one-third of the college program. The student preparing to teach high school should master one content area in any of the following: broad fields such as social studies; fused areas such as physical sciences; or single areas such as mathematics, foreign language, art, or physical education and health.

The rationale for this requirement is to help high school teachers prepare themselves intellectually for the very bright students in their classes who will be seeking additional, in-depth knowledge of a subject.

High school teachers also will have students who need remediation and/or an infusion of motivation. Though these students are found throughout the school system, high school may represent the last opportunity to help them. The high school teacher who has expertise in both an academic field and in motivational skills can be very effective in such cases.

Those preparing to teach middle/junior high school should select two areas of concentration and divide preparation equally between them. This will prepare them for more than one content area, as middle schools often require, and for the scope of the junior high curriculum, which encompasses several content areas. It also helps the teacher satisfy the diverse interests of that age level.

These teachers will build their two-area specialty upon their basic studies. It is also expected they will strengthen their academic preparation through individual effort, continued study, and inservice and teaching activities.

Those preparing to teach elementary school must be trained in a still wider variety of subjects. They may acquire the breadth of content they need by building their areas of concentration on the basic studies

19

component. Assuming the candidates are competent college students, there is every reason to expect that four or five college courses in each of four broad areas will prepare them to teach children in the five- to 10-year-old age range.

The remaining one-third (approximately) of the undergraduate preservice program should be devoted to pedagogy, with requirements completed normally within three years. The preferred pattern would be to complete one year in the basic studies area, and then begin the pedagogical sequence concurrently with the completion of the remaining basic studies work and the area of concentration. When students complete their four years of basic studies, academic major, and pedagogical requirements, they should be eligible for the undergraduate degree and a provisional license to teach.

This Commission does not mean to imply that most institutions do not conform to the above format; however, it does recommend some substantive changes within this structure.

The three-year undergraduate portion of pedagogical preparation should be designed primarily to prepare teachers to perform in the classroom, defined here as any school setting where instruction and learning take place. Thus, "classroom" might be a laboratory, studio, or auditorium, and involve one or several teachers in self-contained or team situations. Certain courses and experiences aimed at preparing teachers to be effective in the classroom should be part of pedagogical programs but are not typically included in all preparation programs, despite their effectiveness.

The most glaring omission lies in the failure to provide laboratory courses necessary to train teachers to become effective diagnosticians. The driving force behind professional preparation, after all, must be the development of conceptual thinking and the application of professional skills. Translated, this simply means that teachers must be able to classify events according to type, analyze situations they are faced with, and be able to use a repertoire of skills (materials, methods, etc.) to "treat" any problem. To do this, they must understand pupils as well as content. They must be able to recognize cues or symptoms indicating certain conditions. They must also learn the technical language of the profession, enabling them to communicate more precisely and efficiently through the knowledgeable use of such terms as questioning, probing, and wait-time.

Most undergraduate programs are seriously flawed in that they fail to provide education students with laboratory facilities. Teacher education should no longer expect students to acquire pedagogical knowledge through passive classroom learning, just as no science instructor would expect science students to learn without manipulating the objects, specimens, measurements, and analysis that go with scientific inquiry.

This is not to say that teacher preparation has not recognized the importance of laboratory experience; student teaching or internship programs have been around for a long time providing excellent experience. However, the burden for furnishing teacher candidates with opportunities for experience cannot rest entirely on a single student-teaching course taken near the end of a program. This is also not to say that many institutions don't provide or require much more field experience. It is to say, however, that if students had laboratories to "try out" the content of courses, they would be able to engage in active learning throughout their preservice study.

The Commission recommends that every course in the pedagogical area have a laboratory component, and that students have access to two kinds of laboratories—called, for discussion purposes, the Teacher Development Laboratory and the Technological and Materials Laboratory. The former would help students learn to work with people (pupils, peers, and teachers), and the latter to work with materials—particularly curriculum materials, computers, and audio-visual equipment. Neither laboratory should be restricted to the physical setting of the college or university, but the use of school facilities should be considered highly desirable.

It is the view of this Commission that the substance of preservice programs will be altered drastically in a positive sense when every course is tied to the reality of the schools and the utilization of materials and technology. This requirement will give all courses an aspect of performance and timeliness that will enliven content, improve professional stature, and force colleges and universities into programs that work.

Though some members of this Commission have had some prior experience with the use of laboratories, it fell to David Berliner (1987) to outline some of the activities and expectations that evolve when making laboratory courses out of the traditional format. The following statements are excerpted from Berliner's suggestions and embellished by Commission recommendations.

*Simulations and Gaming.* Teacher educators should be thinking about building computer simulations with videodiscs. Commanders of merchant ships, business executives, and the military have successfully used simulating and gaming techniques to learn their skills. So too can novice teachers benefit from guided practice with simulated students, which would help them acquire a working repertoire of skills for managing and organizing instruction, and better prepare them to enter a classroom.

*Observation Exercises.* Laboratories should have inexpensive but carefully chosen libraries of teaching performances to enable novice teachers to observe and code teaching. If part of teaching is creating learning environments, then a set of skills for observing and analyzing learning environments is necessary. It would seem that a standard set of lessons to observe, code, categorize, analyze, and discuss would be as necessary a part of teacher training as the use of a pond is for the training of novice biologists.

*Protocols.* A protocol is a record of an event or transaction. Protocols in teaching are materials for interpretation and diagnosis. Prospective teachers must learn to interpret human behavior in terms of a set of sophisticated concepts drawn from various fields and disciplines that are relevant to the teacher's task. Getting beyond everyday experience means learning concepts to help organize the complex and dynamic world of the classroom. Protocols could portray teacher performance, student behavior, differences between concrete and formal operations, child development, and so forth.

*Models and Cases.* Complex model lessons could be shown as case examples. The power of a case study is that it illuminates both the practical and the theoretical. Three types of cases may be identified: *precedents,* which capture and communicate principles of practice or maxims; *parables,* which convey norms or values; and *prototypes,* which exemplify theoretical principles. (A good prototype would be a particularly effective school.) All of the major characteristics found in the literature on effective schools could be illustrated through interview and videotapes of actual school activities.

*Practice.* Laboratories could be used for practice. We have a growing body of knowledge showing that experts respond automatically, with appropriate routines, to professional responsibilities. Education students can be trained to play classroom pupil and teacher roles, practicing the teacher responses until they are in accord with the norms for handling common student behaviors. If we would interweave this skill-training into discussions of how such skills fit more conceptually complex phenomena, it would be very useful in training teachers. Education students can imitate patterns more accurately and retain the ability to give skilled performances themselves when they have an adequate conceptual system to draw on.

*Mediated Learning Experiences.* Laboratories should be places that employ articulate, expertly qualified teachers or mediators to talk to novice teachers about all aspects of their learning. The mediator would skillfully induce interaction between learner and environment by influencing the learner's responses, impulses, tempo, and rhythm through modeling, reinforcing, telling, interpreting, and any other effective form of teaching.

The shift from predominantly vicarious learning to the attainment of knowledge through classroom instruction, laboratory experiences, and direct contact in the schools calls for investment in teacher education beyond that presently provided by university budgets. University support for teacher education pales in comparison to the support given other departments. This is reflected in the allocation of materials, number of students per class, and the ratios of students to instructors for student teaching supervision. The importance of quality programs as an incentive cannot be minimized if teacher education is to attract quality students to the profession in time to alleviate, if not solve, the impending teacher shortage crisis.

## CONCLUSION

T eacher education programs can be improved without total disruption of present systems, but not without major alterations. This calls for action on the part of the critical sectors of society, i.e., the legislative, business, and community representatives who are in a position to make a difference. The profession must improve incentives and working conditions for teachers, and provide better salaries, differentiated opportunities for superior teachers, and school environments that treat teachers in a professional, dignified manner. All ethnic and racial segments of society must be included in the teaching profession but intensive recruitment of the best is preferable to mandated quotas.

Teacher education programs must be maintained and strengthened in existing colleges and universities through four- or five-year programs that may vary according to institutional resources. It is more productive to improve existing programs than to abolish them. The view that fewer institutions should prepare teachers and that teacher education be removed from undergraduate programs is probably a legitimate concern, and might ultimately be the solution to the quality and quantity issue facing the profession. But until there is more evidence and less risk in such a proposal, this Commission cannot support the abolition of four-year undergraduate preparation programs. Teacher education needs to be revised so that present theory and research knowledge is utilized more effectively.

The Commission also recommends the development of pedagogical laboratories where prospective teachers can acquire knowledge about theory and research, practice skill development in technological and substantive areas, and make the successful transition from the pre-service program into the real life of the classroom.

The nation will suffer drastically in the immediate and distant future unless a) schools effectively prepare the next generation to assume responsibility for maintaining and improving society and b ) the educational system effectively copes with such problems as high drop-out rates, sub-minimal academic performance for a high percentage of today's youth, lack of interest in teaching on the part of those with the most potential, attrition from the ranks of teachers, and an impending teacher shortage. The ills of society cannot be dumped on the schools but the prevention of those ills can often be based in the schools. The opportunity to take a large step forward by supporting improved teacher education and teaching conditions is present. The responsibility of replacing about half of today's teachers with new professionals in the next few years can be either an impressive success or an abysmal failure. The task of making the right recommendations rests with those in a position to make significant decisions. It is the hope of this Commission that its recommendations will help provide the guiding principles and foundation for the right decisions.

# II

## The New America For
## The Third Millennium

I n a dozen years, we will enter the third millennium. The preceding 2000 years have been years of dramatic and unbelievable human change. Three-fourths of that period transpired without knowledge of the existence of the Americas; all but 300 years occurred before the industrial revolution; and only 2 percent during the post-industrial era, the period of most rapid change, or what Toffler calls "the third wave." The process of change continues to accelerate daily and will become more intense as we enter the third millennium.

Even in the short lifespan of those of us who read this document, the compounding rate of change has been overwhelming. Rapid advances in transportation and communication, the potential for world tension and destruction, the potential for the betterment of humankind, and now in more recent years, the changing demographics of American society challenge us in ways that we could not have imagined possible in the year 1 A.D.

Most of these changes affect schools and the education of teachers. Among the most relevant are America's shifting ethnicity, the changing nature of the American family, and the internal and external forces (such as technology, a shrinking world, and changing values) impacting on demographics in our society.

### CHANGING DEMOGRAPHICS, CHANGING EDUCATION

M ost of the reports focusing on the improvement of education don't say much about the ways in which quality and access to the teaching profession are interrelated. In the minds of many people, including state legislators, access and quality are like two sides of a teeter-totter. They argue that the focus has been primarily on access, which is why quality has decreased. They state, therefore, that for the future, raising quality must be stressed, even at the expense of access. Their logic implies that to improve quality, access must be narrowed.

This thinking characterizes some national and state-level recommendations that imply that educational improvement is toward one direction or the other, and that an excess in one direction can be

25

eliminated simply by de-emphasis. The answer is obvious: access can be broadened and quality improved at the same time. The two approaches are not mutually exclusive.

Educational reforms seem to occur in cycles, but the importance of regular and consistent assessment can hardly be over-emphasized. Such analysis provides the basis for projecting future directions. Demography, as a part of environmental analysis, for example, is a highly important factor in helping decide what must be done if the quality of education and the supply of teachers are to be consistent with our needs.

Most notable among the demographic changes in the United States in recent years are:

1. The number of single-parent families and working mothers has risen sharply while family size has decreased.
2. The 80 million households in the United States today are more varied sociologically than the nuclear family of a quarter-century ago.
3. America has become grayer. In 1985, we became a nation with more persons over 65 than teenagers. The number of people over 100 years of age in the United States—30,000—will probably double or triple in the next 10 years.
4. Previously sharp differences in sex roles are becoming blurred. Forty percent of supermarket shoppers are male; 30 percent of General Motors car customers are female.
5. The South and Southwest populations are increasing while some sections of the North are facing rapidly declining populations. Nevertheless, 50 percent of the U.S. populace lives in the Eastern time zone.

## CHANGES IN FAMILY STRUCTURE

In a recent study, researchers at Harvard and MIT (*The Nation's Families: 1960-1990*) predicted that the traditional family will become even rarer by 1990. Major changes have taken place in the ways Americans live together. In 1955, 60 percent of the households in the United States consisted of a working father, a housewife mother, and two or more school-aged children. In 1980, that previously typical family could be found in only 11 percent of American homes, and in 1985, in only 7 percent—an astonishing change. Just think of what this means for schooling.

In *All One System,* Harold L. Hodgkinson points out that only 7 percent of the children who attend American schools live in households consisting of a working father, housewife mother, and two or more school-aged children. A large and growing segment of the population has no direct family involvement with schools. Of the 80 million households today, almost 20 million consist of people living alone. According to the census, 59 percent of the children born in 1983 will live with only one parent before reaching age 18—this now becomes the normal childhood experience. Of every 100 children born today:

- 12 will be born out of wedlock;
- 40 will be born to parents who divorce before the child is 18;
- 5 will be born to parents who separate;
- 2 will be born to parents of whom one will die before the child reaches 18;
- 41 will reach 18 "normally."

The United States today is confronted with an epidemic increase in the number of children born outside of marriage, 50 percent of whom are born to teen-aged mothers. Although the percentage of black teen-aged girls who have children out of wedlock is higher than that of white girls, comparisons with other nations indicate that a white teen-aged female in the United States is twice as likely to give birth outside of marriage as in any other nation studied. The situation is most frightening with very young mothers. Indeed, every day in America, 40 teen-aged girls give birth to their third child. To be the third child of a child is to be very much "at risk" for the future. There is a particular aspect of the situation that is vital: teen-aged mothers tend to give birth to children who are premature. This means that about 700,000 babies annually are almost certain to be either educationally retarded, or "difficult to teach." This group is entering the educational continuum in rapidly increasing numbers.

## AMERICA'S SHIFTING ETHNICITY

The United States is a nation of 14.6 million Hispanics and 26.5 million blacks. By 2020 A.D., there will be 44 million black and 47 million Hispanic Americans. The total U.S. population in 2020 A.D. will be about 265 million people, a small increase over our current 238 million—and more than 91 million of that figure will be minority. Around the year 2000, just 12 years away, America will be a nation in which one of every three will be non-white. The trends in birth rates among "white" as one category and "black and other" as another are very revealing. In 1955 there were 3,485,000 white births and 613,000 births to black and other categories. This meant that the number of black and other births was 17.6 percent of the number of white births. In the years that followed, the percentage increased as follows:

|      |       |
|------|-------|
| 1960 | 18.2% |
| 1965 | 20.4% |
| 1970 | 20.7% |

|      |       |
|------|-------|
| 1975 | 23.2% |
| 1980 | 24.6% |

(*Statistical Abstracts of the United States* 1986.)

As these figures show, the nation's responsibility to ensure equal opportunity and access for all becomes even more crucial in sustaining economic and social stability.

## REGIONAL POPULATION CHANGES

T he national decrease of about 13 percent in the number of public school students in the 1970-1980 decade breaks down to zero decline in about 12 "Sun Belt" states, and over 25 percent in some "Frost Belt" states. As a result, there will be two major educational agendas for the next decade: 1) Planning for growth (kindergarten through graduate school) in 12 states; and 2) planning for continuing decline in secondary school populations in most of the rest. These projections would change if retention rates change appreciably.

Concurrent with this regional migration is a hastening flight from metropolitan areas. Within the last four years, over six million people over four years of age have moved to non-metropolitan areas. Although cities have continued to grow, a more rapid annual rate of population increase occurred in non-urban areas. As predicted, central cities lost population and suburbs gained; more blacks are now moving to the suburbs, and blacks are now 6 percent of the suburban population, but most blacks continue to live in central cities. Hispanics, as well as single men and women, most frequently reside in central cities, too. If such trends continue, will society be more segregated by the year 2000, or will there be ways to bring diverse groups together without physical proximity? And what implications will all of this have for schooling?

A summary of what appears to be the consequences for schooling with respect to demographic changes includes the following:

1. More of the children in our public schools will come from minority backgrounds, single-parent families, and poverty households.
2. There will be a larger number of children who were premature babies, leading to more learning difficulties in school.
3. More "latch-key" children and children from "blended" families of remarried parents will be enrolled in public schools.
4. More children will be born to teen-aged mothers.
5. The percentage of workers with a college degree will increase.

These five consequences are based on low-inference information which makes their prediction highly accurate. The remaining consequences are likely to occur unless unforeseen developments alter their direction:

28

6. A continued drop nationwide in the number of high school graduates can be expected, particularly in the Northeast.
7. A major increase will occur in the number of part-time college students and a decrease of about one million full-time students. (Of approximately 12 million students, only about two million are currently full-time, on-campus residents 18-22 years of age.)
8. A continuing increase will take place in the number of college graduates who will get a job requiring no college degree (currently 20 percent of all college graduates).
9. There will be major increases in adult and continuing education outside college or university settings through business, government, non-profit organizations such as United Way, and for-profit "franchise" groups, such as Bell and Howell schools and the Learning Annex.

## THE CHALLENGES TO EDUCATIONAL LEADERSHIP

What does the preceding array of statistics and figures mean for those who provide leadership and instruction in school systems, and those who are responsible for the future education of teachers? The orderly, sequential patterns of the past have weakened under the onslaught of change efforts resulting in the current state of uncertainty in education. The situation demands strong leadership at the school and district levels if schools are to emerge with a higher level of quality and more productive standards than ever before. In addition, the preparation of teachers will need to be refocused to meet the needs of a changing society, for the demographic shifts that are underway will produce a significant range of new concerns and new quality standards, including:

1. An increased awareness of diverse populations with different language orientations. With American urban education becoming increasingly Spanish-oriented, it will become a requirement of teachers, especially of the young, to have a strong sensitivity to languages in addition to English.
2. An expanded use of computer tools to facilitate learning, as well as to communicate knowledge and information. Computer literacy will become more necessary and commonplace.
3. The development of additional day-care capacities, since larger numbers of students will come from households with single parents, working parents with no after-school child care arrangement, and "blended" families.
4. Further analysis of the impact of television and other means of technology that play a role in teaching. (More and more of what students learn today is not acquired at school or university.)
5. Re-examination of teacher retirement arrangements, in view of

29

increasing longevity, and decreasing numbers of teachers. A rich source of professionals may be found in those who have taught for many years, and who with incentives would return, or those who come from other occupations and wish to explore a second career at a different stage in life.

6. Increased opportunities for the use of part-time professional personnel in schools. People such as qualified parents, retirees, and professionals from fields other than education may be available for such employment.

7. The recruitment of qualified minority students as teachers in comprehensive campaigns led by minority leaders.

8. Provision of a wider range of experience in teacher preparation programs, in order that student teachers not complete their entire internship in schools isolated from the diversity of American society. All prospective teachers should spend a portion of their internships in linguistically and culturally different environments.

To conclude, our changing demography requires strong leadership and dynamically creative teacher education programs in American society. Perhaps the most significant consideration will be a deep sense of commitment to quality education. How one achieves commitment is difficult to explain. Schools are a direct reflection of their leaders, their principals, and the quality of their teachers. The commitment, concerns, and sense of purpose of these individuals are key factors in determining the direction in which schools move. The changing demographics of American society make it especially important to strive toward a national commitment to quality in education, and to shaping a future that will be more productive than our past.

# III

## Teacher Supply and Demand

Within the next decade, the demand for teachers will outstrip the supply. Several known factors and a large number of unknown variables will bring about this event. One would think this emergency would warrant federal and state intervention to solve the problem. However, such intervention does not appear imminent even though the shortage will occur sooner than expected in some inner-city and isolated rural districts, and in certain specific subject areas such as math, science, and bilingual education.

In recent years there has been a surge of back-to-school stories each fall about the real, imagined, or projected supply and shortage of teachers. This type of investigative journalism has the media looking for someone or something responsible for the problem and then making sure they are put on the evening news or on the *Today* show for three minutes to review the problem and the potential solution. If this individual or organization cannot be found, then those responsible for the lack of good data or information will be grilled as to why the public didn't know about this serious problem earlier.

The teacher supply and demand problem has always been a part of education. At various times in the history of our country there have been shortages, and states have taken corrective procedures, such as the issuance of emergency certificates or calling back retired teachers, as during World War II. Some districts have always had a problem in recruiting enough teachers for the opening of school even when there was an oversupply. Unless the forces creating this problem become a year-round news story, the man on the street, assisted by the media, will view this problem as a back-to-school item that schools and colleges will solve by mid-September each year.

The current version of the supply and demand story centers around an upswing in elementary school enrollment in the late 1980's that will impact high schools and colleges in the 1990's. Also contributing to the problem is an aging or changing work force of teachers leaving the profession in larger numbers each year. Overlaying both of these problems are the changes in society that make selecting a career in teaching less attractive, such as the changing role of women, changes in

31

the family structure, and the explosion of technology and knowledge. A more recent force is the demand by the reform movement that we improve the quality of the teaching force and reduce class size.

## DEFINING THE PROBLEM

### A. The Estimated Demand for Teachers

The demand for new teachers which started to grow between 1981 and 1982 is expected to increase continually into the 1990's and beyond. The factors creating the shortage are increased student enrollment, the demand by reformers for smaller-sized classes, and teachers retiring or leaving the profession for other reasons. The National Center for Educational Statistics (NCES) made the following projections in its 1985 Condition of Education:

> In 1980 the total demand for elementary and secondary teachers in public and private schools was 2,463,000. The projected demand for 1993 is 2,737,000. This represents an increase in demand of about 274,000 additional teachers.

The demand for new teachers each year is calculated by determining how many teachers leave the profession and how many teachers are needed to instruct a growing student population. When calculations are based on these figures, it is possible to determine, on an annual basis, the number of new teachers prepared each year as a percentage of the demand. Using this approach the new supply of teachers was 107.5 percent in 1980 and 122.8 percent in 1981. The drop during the next two years to 88.8 and 89.0 percent was offset by an increase to 102.1 percent in 1984. However, the percentage of demand predicted for the next five years shows a sharp decrease:

| | |
|---|---|
| 1989 | 78.5% |
| 1990 | 73.9% |
| 1991 | 67.6% |
| 1992 | 63.7% |
| 1993 | 63.0% |

The annual average supply of new teachers projected during the five year period from 1989 to 1993 is about 137,000 new teacher graduates. Though some of the factors that make this projection imprecise are discussed later in this section, a broad estimate suggests that approximately 70,000 additional new teacher graduates would be required each year to provide the teaching force required into the 1990's. Further analysis reveals that the greatest shortages will be in the areas of special education, general elementary education, bilingual education, biological and physical sciences, and mathematics.

The demand projections used by NCES are based on a rise in student enrollment, a slight lowering of student-teacher ratios and a constant 6 percent turnover of teachers each year. It is likely these factors will not change appreciably, but a few surprises such as the following could nudge the demand either up or down slightly from these projections:

- The changes in federal tax law under charitable giving could influence donations for private or religious institutions resulting in fewer private schools and more students enrolling in the public schools.
- State or federal governments could adopt a modified or full voucher plan resulting in the loss of state money and students to the private sector.
- A change in the overall economy could influence the amount of money for education. A down turn in the economy could reduce or reverse the drive for smaller class sizes as part of the reform movement, but an economic surplus in states could speed up the process or lower class sizes even more.
- The complex personal variables that determine when a teacher decides to drop out of the profession or take early retirement could be influenced by many factors. Some experts predict that increasing statewide mandates will limit professional autonomy, forcing more and more teachers out of the profession, and probably discouraging recent college graduates from coming in.

## B. The Estimated Supply of Teachers

Making predictions concerning the supply of teachers is more risky than predicting the need for teachers. The pool of available teachers depends almost entirely on personal choice. New graduates, returning teachers, and others who might qualify can all decide at any point to take or not take a job in teaching or to choose another career. The personal reasons for this choice are not easily identified in most surveys.

In addition, a large percentage of teacher education graduates never become teachers. NCES estimates that approximately 146,000 new teacher candidates graduated in 1983. As a percentage of total bachelor degrees granted, the number of new teachers dropped from 34 percent of the total in 1970 to 14 percent of the total by 1983. All these reasons have impelled state policy leaders to call for alternative certification procedures to increase the pool of available teachers. Concern over why students are not choosing teaching as a career has also resulted in calls for higher salaries, career ladder and/or merit pay schedules, and proposals for improving the status of the profession and teacher working conditions.

The reasons why college students do not opt into teaching are difficult to document. It is even more difficult to estimate the size of the reserve pool of qualified former teachers and what it would take to attract them back to teaching.

Mr. Jack Skillett of Emporia State University in Kansas estimates that the elementary teacher pool is exceedingly large and predicts there may never be a shortage in this area. He speculates that many people in the reserve pool will move into and out of teaching, depending on the availability of other higher paying jobs. For example, he sees a relationship between housing industry starts and the supply of teachers. When there's a shortage of shop teachers, it's because the construction of new homes is booming. This might also be true with agri-business jobs and vocational education teachers, and perhaps other positions as well.

## C. The Bottom Line of Supply and Demand

An understanding of the real extent of the teacher shortage problem will depend on more extensive data gathered from individual teachers, individual schools, and school districts. Aggregating these data at the state and national level will allow state policy makers and colleges and universities, as well as individuals, to make decisions leading to a solution of the teacher shortage problem.

National projections on the number of teachers leaving the profession and on the number of new college graduates being prepared for teaching will never be precise. Even estimates of unfilled teaching positions and of the number of state emergency certificates granted will not give a complete picture of the future dimensions of the problem. Better estimates can be made by gathering data at the individual teacher and school building level, particularly of the number of discontented teachers who may be mis-assigned or in an area where they are certified but do not have the desired interest or subject area strength. Combining these data with the number of subject area preparations per teacher per day, the number of teachers picking up extra classes until permanent teachers can be hired, and the number of inadequately prepared substitute teachers all will lead to a better understanding of the hidden teacher shortage problem. Combining these in-school data with those collected by state retirement associations, school district personnel offices and professional associations may help in compiling all the personal data that might indicate future retirement plans, dissatisfaction with current assignments, and other changes that are so difficult to foresee.

Decision-makers cannot tackle the supply problem unless they have

34

precise statistics at least four to six years in advance. They need to know in detail which subject areas will be needing additional teachers, and precisely which geographic areas or school districts will have shortages so severe, for example, that 50 percent of all college graduates in a given period of time would have to go into teaching to meet the need. The declining rate of teacher education graduates who actually become teachers should be a strong signal to the profession to implement aggressive recruiting and incentive programs.

Assuming these predictions are correct, the profession should make it a top priority to tap other sources of teachers. The most obvious source is the pool of former teachers, certified teachers who have never taught, and qualified college graduates who might be interested in a career change.

Again, it is important to state that any attempt to solve the supply and demand problem is feasible only if precise statistical information is available to steer educators and administrators in the right direction.

## POTENTIAL SOLUTIONS

T he elementary and secondary schools of our land are labor-intensive. The organization of schools and the use of teachers as generalists who work with groups of 20-30 students for one hour each day, 180 days a year, have been the subject of reform recommendations for decades. The coming teacher shortage may merely provide a new incentive to question some of these prior operating assumptions, or, the shortage may be so intense that it could provide the impetus for significant changes in the structure of education in the United States, as has been suggested by the Carnegie Forum on Education and Economy.

Possible solutions to the teacher shortage include the following.

### A. Technology

Technology could erase school and state boundaries and other artificial lines that contribute to the teacher shortage. Finding teachers who were willing to move to isolated rural areas, one of the most likely places for a teacher shortage, has always been a late-August administrative nightmare. The use of instructional television, satellite technology, video tape recorders, two-way communication lines, and other means of technology might allow isolated school districts to make use of outstanding teachers in urban school districts, colleges, or universities. It may also be possible to use experts in business and industry to help bring to rural areas what many urban and suburban districts take for granted.

35

## B. Foreign Teachers

A number of school districts in the United States have already started to meet teacher shortage areas by hiring teachers from foreign countries. Canada and Western Europe, e.g., have an oversupply of teachers who have been well-trained, speak fluent English and only need to become acclimated to American social mores to facilitate their adjustment to public school teaching in the United States. Hiring teachers from this pool will, of course, provoke basic questions concerning our certification process and teacher training programs. It may also introduce some welcome new attitudes concerning respect for teachers, breadth of subject matter, and teaching methods. The number of teachers from this pool will probably never be large but it should, nevertheless, add an interesting mix to both school district and teacher training activity.

## C. Certification Changes

Alternative certification programs, temporary certificates, and emergency certificates, are all solutions that have been used to help alleviate teacher shortages. The recommendation to phase out the undergraduate major in education, using the Bachelor of Arts degree as a starting point for teacher training, may set the stage for larger use of alternative certification methods. States that have experimented with this program—New Jersey, California and others—have had mixed success. If this solution is to be used, an effective means of recruiting and retaining candidates in the profession will have to be found. In some ways this may be the same problem as training and recruiting teachers in any regular cycle.

## D. Public Opinion

Mobilizing public opinion to support practicing teachers as well as those about to choose to enter teaching will be an important step in helping to solve the crisis. Changing the negative image teaching has developed will be a formidable task. Until the public recognizes that the lack of good classroom instruction affects every occupation and business, and the economy as a whole, the teacher shortage will probably not be solved. It has been recommended there be more publicity about the positive aspects of teaching, particularly from former teachers who have returned to the profession; people who have selected teaching as a midlife career change; or respondents to polls that portray teaching more favorably than vocal critics do.

The elevation of teaching to a status that will attract and retain a fair share of the nation's most competent people requires collaboration with society and reconstruction within the profession. These reforms must move forward before teacher education programs can attract, prepare, and place large numbers of highly qualified teachers in the nation's schools.

# IV

## Technology
## and Teaching

The world has been irreversibly altered by the technological revolution still in its infancy. Despite the progress that remains to be made, current developments have already thrust today's society far beyond the limits established a mere generation ago. The fascination with this new age is shared by many Americans, who regard technology as a measure of the good life.

While technology attracts and drives much of American society, some sectors have been influenced less than others. Schools, for example, have been comparatively unaffected by information-age technology. For teachers, textbooks remain the dominant technology.

Why have schools been so slow to adopt modern technology? Surely, there are many reasons, but here are a few important facts. 1) *Lack of research and development money.* Public schools lack adequate funds to support research, development, and capital improvement. There may be money for new buildings but very little for instructional equipment. 2) *Fuzzy productivity indices.* Because the goals of schooling are vague, it is difficult to justify capital investment for productivity purposes. Will modern technology enable schools to educate more students, in less time, with greater results, at lower cost? Such a question may seem reasonable to an industrial economist, but it sounds strange to an educator. Teachers wish to prepare individual students to maximize their own unique potential. What does such a goal mean in terms of productivity and does technology have a role to play? 3) *De-humanization of schooling.* Teachers react negatively to proposals that appear to de-personalize instruction. ("Dial-a-prayer" may meet a need, but it is not a substitute for a deep religious experience.) Drill-and-practice exercises on a micro-computer may enhance students' basic skills, but teachers do not count drill-and-practice lessons as valuable as instruction promoting higher-level thinking skills.

Yet, educators are both attracted and repelled by the prospects of instructional technology. In theory, why can't technology relieve teachers of tedious tasks as it has other professionals such as lawyers and physicians? Might technology enhance professionalism or undermine it?

Could teaching be more interesting and learning more fun through effective use of technology? These are questions teachers ponder, but to date the answers have been unpersuasive. It may be that teachers have trouble devising ways they might use technology in their own work. Would they do the same things they do now? Would schools be different somehow if access to technology were no longer an issue?

The following scenario may help readers imagine how instruction could be different in a technologically rich environment, in contrast to the conditions currently present in most schools. The scenario is constructed around a "typical day" in the life of a hypothetical social studies teacher in a small-town high school in Lawrence, Kansas. Clearly, many other scenarios are possible; this one is offered because social studies is not a subject one would ordinarily give first priority to in the application of instructional technology. The story depicted here is not true; names and events are contrived. But neither are many of the elements false. There is a Lawrence High School, and a well-publicized team teaching project did begin there about 25 years ago. Moreover, each of the examples of instructional technology is possible now, and to one degree or another is in use somewhere in the nation.

## A DAY IN THE LIFE OF HOWARD MULLINS

*7:15* "Thank God, I have an easy day," thought Howard Mullins, as he backed his car out of his garage, contemplating the busy weekend he'd had, one Monday morning in Spring 1987. Mullins is the lead teacher of American Government and chairman of the Social Studies Department at Lawrence High School. "It was a fantastic weekend, but not very good for rest or preparing for Monday classes. When I had the idea for a 25th anniversary celebration for the school team teaching project, I did not imagine it would be so successful. Imagine! More than 200 came. Then, to top it off, we showed the videotape with greetings from former students and teachers who are now scattered all over the world. How exciting it was to sense the impact the project has had on so many people.

"Really," Mullins mused, "I wonder how we were able to do anything 25 years ago, before we had the technology now available to us. Then, the overhead projector was a big deal. Except for some filmstrips, 16mm films, and overhead transparencies, we depended totally on textbooks and the books of readings we produced ourselves. No computers, no VCR, no teleconference, and no video disc—how did we do it?"

*7:45 Mullins arrives at his department office.* Mullins turns on his computer and calls up his electronic mail. It requires more time than usual this morning to read his mail because there are more than a dozen

39

messages from teachers at various schools across the nation who could not attend the weekend reunion but wanted to send congratulations. A few messages require answers. Principal Marker reminded him that textbook orders for next year were due at the end of the month. Professor Ehman, a social studies methods instructor at the University of Kansas, asked if his social studies methods classes could observe small-group discussions on Tuesday afternoon. (Mullins had worked out an agreement with Ehman two years before to install remote control television cameras in Lawrence High School social studies classrooms in order that those university students preparing to teach could observe high school classes from their university classrooms.) Now, Mullins sends Professor Ehman a menu of the programs planned for an entire week, and Ehman chooses from the observation list the experiences he believes will most benefit his teacher education students. The demonstration lessons are beamed live into the university classroom. Ehman also tapes most lessons in order to construct "Highlight Tapes" that he can use later for showing both good and bad examples of teaching.

Two of Mullins' colleagues appear. One, John Olson, is a specialist in instructional technology who helps all of the social studies teams on matters relating to the use of technology. He and Bill Pulley, another American Government teacher, are responsible for arranging a live video conference to be broadcast from Washington, D.C., later in the morning. They tell Mullins that everything is set and ask if he has any concerns. While live video broadcasts are conducted frequently—an average of two a month—and have become relatively routine, technical foul-ups can always occur. Mullins is relieved that all is normal and he won't have to create a last-minute replacement lesson for his American Government course.

*8:00    The Costa Rican model United Nations delegation appears.*
Mullins has been working with a group of talented seniors, helping them prepare for the model United Nations conducted at the University of Kansas each spring. Lawrence High School students had so dominated the forum in recent years that university sponsors began to assign them progressively weaker nations to represent. This year they are Costa Ricans. To meet the increased challenge, the students carefully built data bases on each of the nations represented, and with the help of a University of Kansas political science professor, created computer-based, alternative decision models for each of the issues to be considered and voted upon this year. Their purpose in meeting Mullins this morning is to share some ideas for organizing voting blocs among "unaligned nations" around some of the issues prior to the conference opening. By using electronic mail and the fiber optic "highway" the state of Kansas has established, the Costa Rican delegation can be in touch with any other delegations they choose prior to the opening of the model U.N. meeting.

40

*8:30 "Big Brother."* School begins with announcements that are beamed into every classroom through a closed circuit television system. In the past, announcements had been broadcast by public address speakers and ignored by nearly half the students. The use of closed circuit television has improved student attitudes. Student groups either videotape or present their announcements live, often modeling them on well-known, commercial TV advertisements. The student council awards prizes each semester for the most original announcement.

*8:35 First Class Period—World History.* Today, world history sophomore classes are meeting in groups of eight, each led by a student. Eighty-seven students are thus organized into 11 discussion groups. The faculty monitor the performance of each group, offer information, and stimulate further discussion when necessary. The topic today deals with the freedom available to Soviet adolescents compared to that enjoyed by their American counterparts. The world history students have been studying the Soviet Union for two weeks; the question for discussion today will be introduced by an excerpt taken from "Comrades," a current PBS series depicting life in the USSR. One of the world history teachers has edited the tape to provide a 20-minute videotape discussion stimulus. (Before the advent of the VCR, one of the teachers or a student would have made a brief oral presentation to start the discussion. The videotape is more effective.)

*9:30 Second Class Period—American Government.* Mullins is the lead teacher for this course, which has 145 students, divided into two sections.

Today, however, Mullins has little responsibility for the lesson. The class will be treated during this hour to a live interview with U.S. Secretary of State George P. Shultz, arranged by the CloseUp Foundation through the auspices of the C-SPAN television network. Most of the interview will be conducted by CloseUp students actually present in Washington, D.C., but Lawrence students will have the opportunity to pose two questions to Secretary Shultz through an open phone line to Washington. There is a large television projection screen in front of the classroom. As students arrive, they become quickly absorbed in the program, which is already underway in Washington. (Olson has already started videotaping the interview so the class can view the earlier portion later, if they wish.) Shortly, the CloseUp host announces that they are ready to take questions from Lawrence High School. The students ask two questions, both relating to American foreign policy in Central America. One of the questions was prepared by the morning class, the second by the afternoon class. It was exciting for the students to present their questions directly to the U.S. Secretary of State, and be able to observe his demeanor as he responded.

*10:30 Home Room.* When not pre-empted by various claims on its

41

time, home room is devoted to a half hour of study or individual counseling. Under the Lawrence High system, each teacher counsels about 30 students and, except for rare cases, keeps the same students throughout their three years (sophomore, junior and senior) there. As a result, each teacher knows his/her counselees very well by the time they graduate. Lawrence Public Schools maintain a comprehensive, computerized data base on each student. The file contains records extending through a student's entire tenure in the Lawrence school district, including grade reports, diagnostic and achievement test scores, counseling notes, and other materials, which are brought up to date on a monthly basis. Each student file also contains an "Individual Education Plan," which Mullins uses in counseling his 30 students. He points out their weak areas in various subjects, and suggests what can be done to overcome deficiencies and improve skills. Special services are available beyond regular classes for students who need help.

Mullins remembers how difficult it was to maintain records before the development of electronic data bases, and before each teacher was equipped with his/her own computer terminal, with access to all student records. The Special Services Department has also been enhanced by the equipment and software available for individual students to use at school or at home. And the preparation of end-of-semester reports for parents has been greatly simplified since most of the work can be done by laser printer.

Students who are not attending club meetings or meeting with Mullins are free to do their own homework. Each classroom has three microcomputers available for student use. They are networked so that students can connect to the library, special services, or other classroom teachers. They can also connect to students operating micros in other rooms, which often contributes more to romance than intellectual growth if Mullins fails to pay attention to what is going on.

*11:00   Third Class Period—World History.* This world history class, like the earlier one, is engaged in peer-led, small group discussion. Mullins has agreed to help monitor the discussions this hour as he did during the first class period. However, since he saw the videotape from "Comrades" during the first period, he uses the first half of this class period to respond to his "mail"—electronic and otherwise. He makes telephone calls to those who are available to answer the telephone and leaves electronic messages for others. Among other items of business, he sends electronic notes to all social studies department members, reminding them of their meeting that afternoon, and outlining a tentative agenda of topics for discussion. He also sends the school librarian a list of books, articles, and videotapes he wants placed on reserve for his next American Government unit.

*12:00   Fourth Class Period—Lunch Hour for Mullins.* Rather than going to the teacher's dining room, Mullins is having lunch in his office today. He does this two or three times a week as it provides an opportunity for him to catch up on other tasks. Today, he has scheduled a conference call with 12 American Government teachers from other high schools scattered between Portsmouth, New Hampshire, and Phoenix, Arizona. Mullins and the other teachers use the last three weeks of each semester to engage their students in a program called "Inter-Nation Simulation." The simulation was created at Northwestern University in the late 1950's and was first used at Lawrence High School in 1960. Over time, other American Government teachers began to use it, or modified versions of it. Five years ago, Mullins proposed that a group of high schools play it together, with each school representing one of the "nations." Decisions made each day are recorded electronically and computer-analyzed. At the end of a day, each school is informed by its own computer of the consequences each "nation's" decisions have had upon all of them, individually. "National leaders" can communicate regularly by electronic mail and at least once during the three-week simulation period student leaders are permitted to hold a "summit," using video conferences. Mullins has found the Inter-Nation Simulation to be a terrific learning experience and an excellent way to hold the attention of seniors during the last three weeks of a semester. Today's teleconference session is for teachers to resolve several issues and to discuss new variables to be included in the simulation.

One day each month, Mullins uses the lunch hour to conduct a teleconference with a political science professor at the University of Kansas and 15 other high school American Government teachers around the state. Some of Mullins' students have enrolled in his American Government course for university credit, requiring special readings and assignments. The cooperating teachers discuss Mullins' course with the professor once a month.

In the past, Mullins has also used the lunch hour to pursue televised graduate courses from the University. This has proven to be a convenient way to learn, earn graduate credit, and also renew his teaching license.

*1:00 Fifth Class Period—American Government.* Mullins shows his afternoon class a videotape of the George Shultz interview, but the students are not as interested as the morning class was. It is more fun to be "live." Nevertheless, the class takes satisfaction in watching the Secretary of State answer the questions posed on their behalf.

Mullins tries to get as much benefit as possible from the session by asking the class to analyze the interview and render judgments regarding the students' questions and the Secretary's responses. Mullins had prepared these and other questions during the morning session to help the students draw more from the interview than they might otherwise have.

*2:00  Sixth Class Period—American History.* As department chair, Mullins makes it a point to visit each class as frequently as possible. Today, he decides to attend an American History lecture being given by a student teacher, Jill Russell, who is assigned to the social studies department. He is particularly interested because she is using material from the *Video Encyclopedia* recently purchased by the school library. (The *Video Encyclopedia* contains authentic film in videotape and video disc format of important people and events from 1895 to the present.) The subject is the civil rights movement of the 1960's, and Jill has incorporated some film coverage of the major civil rights leaders of the 1960's.

Mullins takes notes on the lecture using his portable microcomputer so he can later offer Jill advice on teaching techniques during a follow-up session. Despite Jill's nervousness, her lecture was well organized and the students seemed very attentive. Her skill in providing context and analysis while weaving in brief, authentic film excepts of Martin Luther King Jr., Stokely Carmichael, and other civil rights leaders made the lecture powerful and interesting. He decides she has done a good job.

*3:15  Social Studies Department Meeting.* The members of the department meet whenever necessary but at least once a month. Today, the agenda is as follows:

1. Report on the status of the Mastery Testing Program. The Social Studies Department maintains a large bank of test items covering every unit taught for each course. Students who miss a test or perform poorly on the first administration of a test may draw a computer-selected alternative test that covers the same material. For most units, the department's "bank" of test items is sufficient so that students can take four different tests on the same material without seeing the same item again.

2. Report on Newly Available Data Bases. The Social Studies Department has been slowly acquiring pre-packaged, commercial data bases that faculty can use for instruction. Because funds are limited, the department must be selective about what it chooses. The report today is presented by a faculty member who has reviewed a number of newly available data bases to determine which ones to recommend for purchase. The department has also been collecting data on the Lawrence community. The Lawrence data are now complete enough to be useful for projecting educational needs, but nevertheless are modified and enhanced on a regular basis.

3. Education Utility. Lawrence High School is a subscriber to services provided by the "Education Utility," a source of instructional software for subscribing schools on a fee basis.

There is a basic monthly cost; thereafter, fees are billed according to how often the service is used. The materials are ordered by school authorities, transmitted by the utility over telephone wires during the night when telephone traffic is light, and stored on arrival in the school's main computer. Later, the materials can be distributed as needed to classroom computers, teacher terminals, and even students' homes for use on their personal computers if they have modems connecting them to the school's main-frame computer.

The Social Studies Department has not made frequent use of the utility but is currently interested in obtaining materials students can use to develop skills and prepare for certain types of exams. Competency exams administered by the state department of education, for example, are drawing more heavily upon historical and geographical, factual-recall-type items for which commercially developed drill-and-practice materials would help students prepare. Certain word processing packages also offer promise of helping students write better papers. Programs that teach outlining, proper footnoting style, correct spelling, and punctuation mistakes have saved teachers time, allowing them to pay more attention to the substance of student themes and essays. Each month the department reviews new products available from the Utility and places orders for those they wish to use or review.

*4:30 Departure for Home.* "I don't know where the time goes," Mullins mused as he walked from the building to his car. "There just isn't time to do everything that must be done."

"I'm not satisfied with the way world history discussion groups were conducted today. Some of the students exhibited poor group-leadership skills. I wonder if Olson could rig some television recorders that could record and analyze some of the discussions with the classes. Our coaches use videotape to improve athletic skills, why can't we do the same for intellectual skills? We have all the equipment we need. All we require is the creativity to make it work for us.

"In any case," he thought, "the day was a lot of fun. It was exciting to watch my students pose questions to Secretary of State Shultz and a delight to watch Jill Russell perform before a large group of students for the first time. Can there possibly be another job as varied or as stimulating as high school teaching?"

A day in the life of Howard Mullins illustrates some of the potential for enlivening and altering the traditional approaches to teaching. All of the techniques utilized are available now. Adaptations and applications of the approaches used by Howard Mullins can be used in most grade levels and subject areas.

Schools will join the technological revolution along with other sectors of society when teachers conclude that teaching is more fun and less stressful, and students learn more with greater joy through the use of technology than without it. Administrators will allocate resources for technology when teachers insist they require it to perform their work properly. Government officials and taxpayers will spend money for technology when they are shown that it improves schools and helps them function better.

Technology, however, will not survive in education if teachers must spend more time preparing for lessons than they do now; if teachers have less time to devote to students than is currently the case; and if technology trivializes the purposes of schooling. If technology is to be the instrument and not the master, then educators must find ways where technology alone can accomplish certain tasks or achieve certain results, particularly the management of tedious busy work that has forced many teachers to leave the profession. Technology can lead to greater productivity in schooling when educators have a better conception of what productivity means for education, and a better understanding of how it can be used and controlled to serve educational goals. Technology also has the potential to rejuvenate the profession by forcing educators to explore new ways to structure schools and organize their own work.

In general, schools are characterized by a flat organizational structure; a teacher's role varies little from the first day of service to the last. Many able teachers grow bored performing the same tasks year after year, and leave teaching to find more challenging careers. Technology offers them the possibility of individualizing instruction and providing group instruction in dramatic ways; technology can also promote a feeling of intimacy even when transmitting instruction to people in remote locations.

In order for education to exploit the full potential of technology, certain steps must be taken. One of the recommendations this report makes is to include laboratory study in preservice courses. Science programs have always provided laboratories to satisfy academic requirements. Teacher education programs should do likewise, and in addition, offer laboratory courses that focus solely on technology. Such a laboratory can provide preservice students with an opportunity to work with equipment, technology, and machinery that will enhance their effectiveness as teachers. The equipment they need to learn ranges from laminating procedures to television, VCRs, and micro-computers, as well as the standard 16mm projectors, overheads, and cassette tapes. The laboratory is not intended to replace direct instruction but to provide a place where students can practice skills taught in the classroom; where they can develop materials to use in presenting example-lessons for peer and instructor review; and where they can learn to blend methods and content in their instructional planning and presentations.

We cannot assume that prospective teachers know how to operate the technical aids available for improving classroom learning. Instruction in the use of a wide range of such aids should be an integral part of their preparation. Some simple aids may require an hour or two to master and others that are more complicated may require one or more courses. Whatever the case, such instruction is well worth the time, effort, and expense. If teachers are familiar with technical aids that will make them more effective, and if they know the material and goals of their content areas well, they are more likely to create better instructional deliveries. And, if they are provided with opportunities to learn about present technology in their preparation programs and are able to adapt to technical change, they will develop into professionals whose careers can be constantly enhanced by the innovations of tomorrow.

# V

# Governance Issues in the Education Profession

School districts, teacher associations and state departments of education are examining and, in many cases, using their authority to implement career ladders, merit pay, differentiated staffing and salary, entry year programs, curriculum change, and teacher preparation requirements. Those who look to the future suggest that schooling may change drastically. The home, equipped with improved technology, may replace the classroom. Community learning centers, for periodic instruction and examination, may replace the schools. Or perhaps teachers will go into private practice. Indeed there will be changes and the profession will endeavor, within this unclear climate, to take a proactive stance. There is a bright future for teacher education and teaching and educators must not separate the two.

However, a serious issue prevails and is basic to the preparation of teachers and the profession as a whole. The question of "who's in charge" plagues the unity badly needed for optimal progress to take place. This issue undergirds the degree to which educators can capitalize on present opportunities and move forward together to develop a profession that offers the effective leadership needed to build the strong schools this nation requires and deserves.

## GOVERNANCE AND CONTROL

Who governs the profession? We could look to the law of the land which asserts that education is the responsibility of the state. This mandate is realized in the establishment of financial support, teacher certification, and minimum standards for schools and teacher education institutions. Yet this simple answer is diluted by the reality of pressure from many constituencies.

The federal programs, although often routed through the states, have held some control over content, operation, and management. Schools have reduced services and eliminated teacher positions because of lack of funds and community support. Local pressure for improved basic skills has imposed restrictions on teachers, the curriculum, and the materials used in classrooms, so much so that teachers have been losing the power to make decisions in the schools. Segments of our society have succeeded in removing certain texts and topics from the school curricula. As schools become disenchanted with teacher preparation programs that do not prepare teachers to "fit in," the gap between preparation and practice grows wider. School systems bypass the colleges and offer intern programs for entering teachers, with inservice classes taught by their own teachers.

Accrediting bodies require schools and colleges to meet their standards. Colleges and universities seek the approval of the National Council for Accreditation of Teacher Education (NCATE) to help maintain their institutions' reputations. Those institutions seeking both accreditation from NCATE and approval from state departments of education are subject to even broader controls. The need to respond to the recommendations of influential national commissions adds yet another control channel.

The reform efforts, as presented in the NCATE redesign, *Tomorrow's Teachers* (the Holmes Group report) and *A Nation Prepared: Teachers for the 21st Century* (the Carnegie report), and other reports, have made demands that cause many in teaching to ask who's running this profession. Many state departments of education, attempting to affirm their leadership, require competency-based education for pupils as well as competency in teacher education. In some instances, the two institutions (schools and colleges) are proceeding without coordinating their efforts. The influence of the Holmes Group report, and more particularly the selection of the research institutions invited to join them, creates predictable fissures in a profession that lacks unity in its governance. Will the "Selected Institutions" dictate programs that make other institutions appear inadequate for the wrong reasons? And who is to say the separatist view is right? Disagreement among institutions over influence, control, and management promotes suspicion of reports generated by self-appointed sub-groups in the profession.

Support for the establishment of a Professional Practices Board to govern teacher education and certify teachers is not universal. Even the idea of such a board infuriates some members of the teacher education faculties. The recent Carnegie action to appoint members to organize the groundwork for such a board does not have full support of the profession. For example, the appointees include the "presidents of the two major teacher unions, a state governor, two state superintendents and a dozen public school teachers." The omission of teacher educators is a glaring oversight.

Union control in school systems that participate in teacher education raises questions of local control. For example, union rotation lists, based on the union's assertion that all teachers are equally qualified to have student teachers, can hinder a college's effort to place its students with the most exemplary teachers. Discrepancies such as this add friction between these two arms of the profession.

The question of who controls teaching and teacher education is not a new concern, but has recently developed new intensity. The problem is that the various groups that strive to improve the teaching profession—state departments of education, unions, accrediting bodies, teacher education institutions, teachers, and teacher educators—all have an independent voice and a vested interest in their own areas of operation. This sometimes leads them to impinge upon the power and authority of the others, giving rise to the issue of who actually controls and governs the profession. While this is not likely to be resolved in the immediate future, selected judgments must be made before long regarding this and numerous other issues within the profession.

Some higher education institutions will provide initial teacher preparation at the graduate level while others will continue to offer it at the undergraduate level. A liberal arts emphasis will continue to be a component in all teacher education, and higher academic standards will likely be established in both programs. Competency assessment for all educators will occur more frequently. Merit pay, career ladders, greater teacher decision-making, and teaming will be found in some schools and not in others. Induction programs will become fairly common across the states, some governed jointly by schools and colleges and others run solely by schools.

Among these many elements lies the potential for conflict for teacher educators. The debate over a national board for a design of nationwide standards and the certification of teachers will continue to cause concern over the issue of governance among teachers, teacher educators, state departments, and other accrediting agencies. Teacher educators, attempting to govern their turfs, will object to a lack of equal representation in present and proposed groups that make recommendations on the education of teachers. The lasting effect of any reforms will depend on the degree to which those persons actively involved in the teaching profession resolve their conflicts, seek agreements, and move forward as a profession, united in purpose, yet respectful of differences.

Where do the actors in this drama begin? The school and college professionals who participate in the preparation of teachers on a regular basis are the initiators. Here there is likely to be considerable agreement on improving clinical field experiences and working relationships, raising teacher salaries and restoring greater teacher decision-making and curriculum control, increasing teacher participation in teacher education curriculum development, and influencing a change in university reward provisions for teacher educators. All the reform recommendations include an urgent call for improved working relationships between schools and institutions of higher education (IHEs) and it is here that the control issue must first be addressed.

## PAST RELATIONSHIPS

T raditionally, schools have provided the settings in which colleges and universities place their teacher education students. In return, colleges have provided supervisors for these students and often small incentives to teachers. Generally, such arrangements are best described as cooperative or collaborative operations. Teacher education institutions depend heavily upon the cooperation extended by the schools for the operation of their field programs, especially in those states that have a history of requiring early and frequent classroom experience. For example, Ohio requires 300 clock hours in school classrooms prior to student teaching, as well as experience in varied urban and suburban settings. Furthermore, Ohio stipulates the field experiences must be integral to the course objectives and supervised by experienced faculty.

An analysis of these student teaching arrangements provides an opportunity to identify some of the concerns that could be addressed by a more unified governance arrangement. For the most part, colleges control the field experiences. School teachers and administrators participate primarily because they believe that learning to teach requires experience in teaching, and they accept responsibility for assisting in the training of future professionals. They may also seek whatever community status accrues as a result of selection. Teachers may also be gratified by the company of a student teacher and the assistance he or she may render in the classroom.

Teachers continue to provide this service year after year though benefits are meager. In some cases, for example, the college faculty may not provide the supervision expected. Teacher education faculty, on the other hand, recognizing that university rewards for this role are seldom great, often place supervision of student teachers low on their lists of priorities. The traditional ivy tower versus the real world controversy is also evident. The host-guest relationship stimulates unrest rather than establishing control. Even when mutually accepted written agreements, specifying role functions and problem-solving strategies exist, true partnerships may not exist.

If efforts to unite the profession are ever to reach fruition, the potential problems over authority and benefits in areas such as student field experiences need attention. What would teachers and administrators consider as their benefits or profits in these relationships? Large honorariums to teachers may raise morale or at least reduce feelings of being used. However, school people tend to see inservice, on-going staff development and shared governance as primary benefits. Reciprocal service might well be a shared profit for both schools and IHEs.

The management model of the Individually Guided Education (IGE) programs initiated in the 70's addressed both the professional growth of schools, their programs, faculty, and students. (When teacher education institutions join with IGE schools, college faculty become working members of the schools' instructional improvement committee, as well as participants in team planning meetings.) Student learning, including pupils and college students, was a shared goal. Teachers often contributed to the design of college instructional courses and modules while college personnel actively participated in school curriculum development. Preservice teachers became members of the differentiated staffing model and instructional team planners.

In districts where leagues were formed, college and school personnel endeavored to clarify and implement the goals of both programs. State departments of education often became actively involved in networking with the universities and schools in this endeavor. Programs of this type were certainly collaborative and when professional goals/benefits were voiced/shared, visible partnerships were realized.

Teacher Corps staff development projects incorporated the principles of shared decision-making; collaboration and governance; delivery systems; and design for the professional development of teachers, administrators, graduate interns, and community members. Networking among the many projects and participants enhanced positive attitudes. However, unlike many endeavors, these projects were adequately funded, and dollars often determined the shared profits.

Some of these activities of the past provide evidence of successfully shared management in the practice and study of teaching. These success stories provide evidence that sharing is possible. However, the profession has a great deal of "unfinished business" to complete in the establishment of unified and cooperative governance and program development.

## EMERGING PRACTICES

National analyses of the problems and needs of the profession stimulate efforts to improve and unite the teaching profession. Teacher Education Advisory Committees, composed of teachers, administrators, and college faculty, serve as excellent models of jointly developed efforts.

A wealth of internship and entry-year induction programs, operating in a variety of configurations, is being implemented and studied. The classroom teacher-in-residence on campus, often with adjunct faculty appointment, is becoming more common. The position of building-classroom-teacher-supervisor of preservice teachers, who works closely with the college program and is financially supported, has been established. Consortia of IHEs and local education agencies are planning and executing staff development programs and shared leadership. School and college partnerships are developing courses to be taught in colleges and schools, and are sharing teacher loads.

Within the present experimental environment, there are unmistakable signs of working partnerships. Formal agreements and contracts are being developed among the cooperating parties in which mutually honored goals are clearly stated, governance and management strategies are delineated, roles and responsibilities are defined, benefits and services are identified, financial responsibilities are written and agreed upon, and on-going operating procedures are described.

Moreover, the benefits generated in these emerging patterns of shared management are clearly an extension of the "helping profession." There is evidence that college and school personnel can work together and help each other. The presence of financially supported classroom teachers on campus as course instructors, department participants, curriculum designers, and college supervisors has provided satisfying rewards in terms of professional exchange and mutual respect, so basic to developing partnerships.

The issue of governance has also been addressed in entry year programs that have been jointly developed, managed, and financed by participating schools and colleges that share the common goal of inducting new members into the profession. The mentor teacher, relieved of the service relationship with the college-based preservice teacher, functions as a colleague and instructor to the school-based entry teacher. Jointly developed curriculum activities and exchange experiences further enhance the bonding of professionals.

The atmosphere is positive at the present time. Partnerships are developing in increasing numbers. Those who work in classrooms teaching children and young adults are finding ways, with the support of administrators, boards, and trustees, to share their time and professional knowledge, and participate in activities that unify those who share a common interest in preparing teachers. However, sustaining and expanding these efforts is a future concern and challenge to be met.

To summarize this chapter, the number of shared practices will increase with continued and improved financial backing. The value of partnership efforts will be studied and successful practices institutionalized with support and endorsement from schools, colleges, state departments, and professional associations.

The education of teachers will remain the primary function of higher education while the teaching of children will be the responsibility of the schools. Each institution will exist in its own political and business environment, although organization and delivery systems may change drastically as a result of recent recommendations.

Clinical experiences for preservice teachers will improve and IHEs and local school districts will begin discussions on the strongly recommended Professional Development Centers. These centers, jointly operated by schools and colleges for the purpose of shared teaching and research as well as preservice and inservice activities, should provide a workable format for shared management and a true partnership for the improvement of the profession. Much will depend on the financial support available for such an effort and on the development of positive attitudes towards school and college structures, so that motivation and personal incentives may be extended to all participants.

The major hope for the future should be that efforts to achieve excellence will not die from fatigue and lack of funding.

# VI

## Schools, Communities, and the Private Sector

It is a rare report on schools that omits the potential relationship between schools and the business and industrial sectors of the nation. But what about the pros and cons of the business-industry-education (B-I-E) linkage? A happy or unhappy trio? Whatever the answer, feelings are strong among governors and educators who regard it as one of the most crucial topics around but see the relationship in different ways. "Almost every governor in the country has run on a platform of job creation and its link to the education system," according to James M. Souby, a National Governors Association official (Johnson 1985).

In view of the many parties and interests involved, the Carnegie Foundation for the Advancement of Teaching has advocated a formation of a Strategic Council for Educational Development to coordinate the efforts and concerns of business, labor, education, government, and other fields, in its book, *Corporate Classrooms: The Learning Business.*

This section will survey five aspects of B-I-E: a) factors stimulating greater business involvement, b) illustrations of diverse aspects of collaboration, c) education and public sector responses and responsibilities, d) guiding principles for effective, desirable B-I-E partnerships, and e) conclusions and recommendations.

### FACTORS STIMULATING GREATER BUSINESS INVOLVEMENT

There are some underlying assumptions that should be kept in mind. B-I-E collaboration is not presented here as the most critical factor in educational reform but it is likely that:

1. Major changes in the nation and world make it impossible and unrealistic for the education community alone to serve the needs of all of the people.
2. There are general and specific roles for which public sector educative institutions, agencies, and organizations should be primarily responsible.

55

3. There are both broad and general roles in which B-I-E should predominate.
4. There are roles in which B-I-E collaboration is on a parity basis, with each partner sharing specific responsibilities determined through negotiation.
5. Certain principles should be followed in assuring that the well-being of society and individuals will be in the forefront of policies and practices.

Thoughtful people in B-I-E have examined the major issues involved in the three-way relationship and have joined in efforts to bring about reforms that would address inherent problems. These major issues and the responses they have produced include:

*The Nature of the U.S. Economy and Society.* Daniel Bell, Alvin Toffler, John Naisbitt, and many others have alerted the nation to the switch in the U.S. economy from manufacturing, mining, agriculture, and other endeavors to one in which knowledge and information production and utilization predominates. Poor education in the current "third wave" economy, to use Toffler's concept, is poor business—it stunts citizenship preparation and individual development, and limits opportunities.

*Education Reform Publicity.* The outpouring of national reports calling for major education reforms has increased awareness of what's involved in building a productive education system. Business and industry (B-I) has seen that it should contribute nationally and within the states. More than 20 national reports from various groups have captured the nation's collective mind; a seemingly endless flow of state and local reports has added momentum to reform action.

*Illiteracy as a Highly Visible National Problem.* Illiteracy is both a personal tragedy and a negative force in the national economy. (Illiterates cannot function well in their personal lives and are ill prepared for B-I positions.) The nation has been shocked to learn that one in five adults (23 million people) is functionally illiterate and that another 40 million are marginally literate. B-I leaders believe there is a direct relationship between illiteracy and low productivity, errors, accidents on the job, high turnover, and other drains on productivity and profits (American Council of Life Insurance 1983). Illiterates in earlier times could perform "take/place/put/lift" jobs; those jobs have declined drastically (Henry 1983).

*Changes in the Ethnic-Racial Composition.* The increasing Hispanic and black population is of concern to B-I. There is an alarming dropout rate among other educational problems that affect many minority students (including native Americans and certain Asian-Americans). Enlightened B-I leaders have taken some affirmative action steps. Many now agree that there is a need for special help for minority students.

56

*Education as an Investment.* Education is now recognized as an investment as well as an expense. There are ways to determine the value of good education. Harder to determine are the costs of ineffective education, both in terms of the individual and the economy. Recognizing the investment side of learning, B-I leaders have become solid boosters of education.

Other examples of B-I-E connections include the Regents reform package for New York which provides credits for out-of-school work experience. Colleges have long awarded undergraduate credits for work experience. Both examples indicate recognition that work can be a source of bona fide learning.

B-I leadership is also very strong on national, state, and local study commissions—a powerful connection (Timpane 1984).

The nation's system of land-grant universities is a prime example of how to blend theory, research, and practice. It is widely given credit for much of the economic well-being of the country, and could be studied for additional applications.

The community school concept has always included collaboration with business and industry, along with other educative institutions, agencies, and organizations. Considerable theory and experience are therefore available for current applications. (A small national organization, the National Community Education Association, continues to bring adherents together to maintain interest and experimentation. Other noteworthy organizations include the National Association for Industry-Education Cooperation and the National Commission for Cooperative Education.) Fantini notes that we have been moving from a school-based system to a community-based system, and when national reform efforts focus solely on school reform, "we are focusing on only one piece of the educational process" (Fantini 1985).

## EDUCATIONAL AND PUBLIC SECTOR RESPONSIBILITIES

Most educational reform efforts have not taken a broad view that weaves institutions into a system for human learning. Instead, they have viewed each institution as separate and unrelated to the broader process of education. Now is a time to reassess our system of education, regroup our educational resources, and systematically link them to support learning for all people (Fantini, *Ibid*).

B-I-E connections, when properly conceptualized, developed, and nurtured, can well meet Cremin's definition of education:

... the deliberate, systematic, and sustained effort to transmit, evoke, or acquire knowledge, attitudes, values, skills, and sensibilities, and any learning that results from the effort, direct or indirect, intended or unintended (Cremin 1980).

B-I-E collaboration is also needed on the college level, where declining federal support for higher education has given philanthropic endeavors from the private sector an even greater significance than in the past. Colleges prize contributions that permit unrestricted use, particularly those such as the university which, pushed for space, built a classroom unit and designated it "New Building," while waiting for a donor to provide a proper name—that of the donor!

Specific programs are also very valuable, such as the drug prevention program funded by an industrialist who provided one million dollars to a university college of education for that purpose. The money will be used to train prospective teachers on how to discourage children from using drugs (*Arizona Republic,* October 15, 1986).

Another example is an industrial fellows program for graduate engineering students—in this case, a large corporation providing support for students of computer-integrated manufacturing. Three-way advantages accrue from the arrangement: for the corporation, a chance to observe prospective employees in on-the-job situations over a 21-month period; for the university, a desirable blending of theory, research, and practice; and for the students, a valuable learning experience and financial support valued at $35,000 (salary, grant, and tuition waivers).

There is also an advantage for the nation. University and corporation officials have noted that the program provides an inducement for Americans to obtain graduate education in the computer field, where more than half the graduates are currently foreign nationals (*Arizona Republic,* September 21, 1986).

In addition to working directly with the education sector, business and industry executives often provide in-house educational opportunities for their employees. These programs are highly diverse and typically situation-specific. They can be highly technical, such as learning how to use a supercomputer to improve company effectiveness; or academic, with courses that could fit into a typical university program, such as psychology, Western intellectual history, and creative writing. Whatever is offered, however, tends to be tailored to a specific assignment or provide preparation for a specific promotion.

In her report, *Corporation Classrooms: The Learning Business,* Nell P. Eurich noted that some $60 billion is spent annually on corporate-run education. That amount is comparable to the expenditures of public and private collegiate institutions. In addition, corporate program enrollments are approaching the same level of colleges and universities (*New York Times,* January 28, 1985).

The Association of Teacher Educators studied a cross-section of B-I in-house education programs (Houston 1986). The analysis presented in

58

their report revealed that:

1. All have training that emphasizes pride in the company as well as skill development.
2. All require uniform procedures.
3. Most have an advanced, centralized training facility.
4. Individual units pay costs of training, regardless of where the training occurs.
5. Employees are expected to continue their education throughout their career.
6. Employees are kept informed of recent developments and future plans of the organization.
7. The enormous costs of employee development have been shown to result in a more effective and efficient organization.

## GUIDING PRINCIPLES FOR B-I-E COLLABORATION

P assow provides eight principles that relate to B-I-E collaboration (Passow 1985).

1. The program has clear educative goals that are congruent with the goals of the schools. The educational objectives to be attained are clear and valid.
2. The program has a curriculum design—a plan for providing the learning engagements and experiences that will help achieve program goals and objectives.
3. The program has selected appropriate pedagogical/instructional strategies for implementing the curriculum.
4. The agency has the personnel and material resources needed to implement the curriculum. These resources are generally more appropriate for the program design than are the resources of the school. (Sometimes the school's personnel and resources are more appropriate.)
5. The nonschool agency's instructional goals either complement or supplement the educational goals of the school.
6. At some stage of program design, the agency and the school engage in joint planning aimed at combining or coordinating their efforts.
7. Educational efforts of nonschool agencies should be subject to appropriate evaluation in order to guide decision-making about program changes.
8. Nonschool educative agencies may provide inservice education for school personnel when such agencies have the resources needed for staff development. The aim of such staff development is to facilitate the integration of school and nonschool educational efforts.

# CONCLUSIONS AND RECOMMENDATIONS

When educators in schools and other settings engage in each other's instruction critically, analytically, and cooperatively, clearly the learners will be the ultimate winners. This is especially so when the nonschool educative agency has the resources for designing educational and instructional activities to engage students in learning more effectively than the school can. The school should use these activities to enrich its own instruction.

Other principles should be considered in conjunction with those of Passow. A program's long- and short-term contributions to its students and to society in general should be examined in the context of political social, and economic considerations. Specific social goals should be juxtaposed with business/industry goals: e.g., equity for all socio-economic classes, races and ethnic groups, sexes and ages, including those who are handicapped. Care should be taken to avoid exploitation of student clients. Diverse learning options should be studied before a particular one is selected. Options should be cost- and time-effective for both B-I-E and the students involved.

Without disputing that schools have primary responsibility for the education of all students, there are some roles that properly call for B-I-E collaboration. When business and industry have a clear superiority in personnel, resources and experience for a particular project or purpose, either in school or other settings, educators should consider the feasibility and desirability of joint programs. After implementation, they should carefully develop and periodically review operating principles to ensure that the well-being of their students is protected and enhanced. Given the size and diversity of the U.S. learning population, the magnitude and rapidity of social and technological change, the cost of personnel and equipment, and other such major factors, B-I-E collaboration is necessary if the U.S. is to become an even greater learning society.

Historically education has provided at least a partially open socio-economic system. Together with the western frontier, an expanding economy, and social experiments such as the GI Bill and Head Start programs, education has facilitated upward mobility for many. A creative B-I-E partnership could reinforce this movement and become an important part of efforts to ensure continuing social and economic access to opportunities, especially for minorities. It also could decrease the dangerous development of "technology-created unemployment" and retard the growth of the "permanent underclass of the unemployable" noted by Clifford (1985) as well as alleviate the existing problem of underemployment.

The public and private sector must become creative in establishing

60

frontiers of the mind and spirit. The economic success of the Japanese has demonstrated what can be done with human resources in the absence of natural ones. The U.S. has both human and natural resources of unbelievable scope. An example of what can be done is taking place in Kentucky, which, in a joint venture with a corporation, has pledged to train and pay workers preparing for work in a new automobile industry (*Lexington Herald Leader,* September 10, 1986).

Educators, faced with change and challenge, alternately chastised and praised, should examine the wide array of options open to them. Lieberman makes a direct assertion that B-I can provide some goods and services more efficiently than the public sector. He conjectures that if educators were freed of some of their business functions there might be more energy available for instructional matters (Lieberman 1986, p. 731). There is nothing new in the argument or in current practice. What is needed is a massive study to determine whether a major move toward privatization is justified. A real test of openness to privatization comes in thinking about contracting out instruction, for example, to Control Data (Lieberman 1986, p. 734).

Educators should join with B-I in considering alternatives to the current practice of gathering tens of millions of students together every day for schooling. Formal schools will always have a place as centers where students can have multicultural experiences; certain kinds of socialization; and group activities, such as music and sports. However, certain circumstances make it possible for much instruction to be given in homes and neighborhood learning centers (institutions, agencies, organizations, and enterprises) by adults who may be available as a result of early retirement, flex hours, company encouragement to work at home, and other such factors. With sufficient incentives, B-I could both develop new technology and improve on existing technology to create near-home and in-home learning systems that would be more economic and efficient than the current system of commuting to sometimes distant schools (Gips and Burdin 1983).

This Commission advocates an open approach to alternatives, which will become more feasible when B-I-E joins its capabilities and experiences together. What, for example, could B-I-E do to address the danger of a new underclass developing for the lack of computer literacy and competence? With encouragement and support from educational systems, B-I might be able to develop a compact, economic learning package that would incorporate a computer, calculator, interactive telephone, facsimile machine, and other technologies. Such a portable study carrel might be checked out for use by students and families, solving the problem of affordability for many.

With awareness, vision, openness, and motivation, B-I-E could establish a team that would include others responsible for educative functions. The responsibilities of the school superintendent, for example, could be broadened so that in addition to leading the schools, this official would also promote and coordinate educational endeavors throughout the community. This would involve working with B-I-E, the press and media, volunteer agencies, the military, correctional institutions, health agencies, religious institutions, private schools, and others (Massanari 1978).

A symbiotic relationship can be enhanced. Sullivan provides an example:

> . . . education-industry partnerships offer an opportunity to keep abreast of state-of-the-art knowledge and developments in rapidly changing subject-matter fields. Today's knowledge explosion and changing social roles intensify the challenge of keeping curriculum content and materials up-to-date in such fields as science, technology, and even career education (Sullivan 1986).

B-I could benefit even more than it presently does from the expertise educators could contribute to the private sector. Universities, for example, have unique capabilities for preparing B-I trainers through their schools of education, and departments of business administration (personnel administration, financial management, and legal concerns), and public relations. Professors from varied departments would also be invaluable (Warnat 1980).

Wirtz provides the test for desirable symbiotic relationships—its value for the individuals as they move beyond the benefits of B-I-E collaboration from kindergarten through graduate school and into adulthood: ". . . some kind of provision for interspersing earning and learning of a living, for interweaving employment and self-renewal, is going to have to be recognized as the essential condition for an effective career as a worker, citizen, or human being" (Wirtz 1975).

# Summary

M uch has been written recently about reforming schools and teacher preparation programs. Some excellent ideas have been expressed, with appropriate attention drawn to the importance of schools and the dangers of ignoring destructive trends in the educational system. This report was written to emphasize the following considerations on which we believe the improvement of schools should be founded.

1. Schools have a rich tradition which cannot be ignored. Though it may be tempting to raze the schools and start over, such an action would not only be unrealistic but unwise. The mistakes and victories of the past provide a history from which today's educators can benefit. Today's schools justifiably rest on basic principles developed in the living laboratory of public schools.

2. Major changes in society require dynamic responses from schools. However, provisions for reforming schools and revising teacher preparation must be based on careful analysis of the foreseeable social and demographic changes in order to better prepare for and serve the future school population.

3. The forthcoming shortage of teachers is both a problem and an opportunity. Some may argue that no shortage exists and the future does not pose serious problems for staffing classrooms. Irrespective of data manipulation to suit either argument, there is a shortage of qualified people from the entire spectrum of population in the United States. The present shortage presents an opportunity to improve recruitment methods and make the teaching profession more representative of the country's ethnic and racial diversity.

4. Productive change must blend business, industry, and schools into a successful team. The responsibility to educate each generation to assume productive roles in society is too difficult for any one entity. The traditional educational institutions must be joined by the expertise and resources of the private sector to ensure a strong future and provide employment security for today's youth.

5. The question of who is in control is an essential issue of professional governance. The teaching profession is confronted with recommendations from sectors of society with limited experience and expertise in education. It is important that teachers' voices become more assertive in determining the important issues of the profession.

6. Reconstitution of the professional, general, and academic subject-

components of teacher preparation is long overdue. There is no need to discuss the proper allocations of time to be dedicated to each of these three areas, or to argue which area is the most important. All three are critical and none can be completely provided during a preservice program. Teachers, therefore, who are part of a "knowledge industry" should expect to continue learning from study and experience.

7. Part of the appeal for those who teach is the opportunity to grow intellectually for a lifetime. Therefore, the profession should not hesitate to establish admission requirements and make teacher education programs exciting and intellectually challenging in order to attract the best and brightest.

# Epilogue

I f schools were performing perfectly, and if educators were totally competent and content, there would be no need for this report. However, the nation is restless about its schools and a good measure of that unsettled feeling comes from those in the profession. Many reports have been written about how to improve America's schools, each generating its own defenders and critics. This report was not written to add another comprehensive view but to focus on the preparation of teachers. Since no recommendations for teacher preparation can be made without considering the present social environment of schools and the foreseeable trends affecting future education, this report has attempted to include all pertinent factors in the presentation of its proposals. Its central purpose is to present recommendations to improve the quality of teaching in the schools of the future. Its major emphasis is on reforming preservice teacher preparation in regard to recruitment, structure, and study programs. Its presentation is based on four generalizations that constitute the foundation for its recommendations: the universal obligation of schools to serve everyone, the need to upgrade the teaching profession, the need to provide pedagogical training for teachers, and the need for school reform to adjust to current and future circumstances.

1. Schools are not doing their job unless they work well for everyone. However, this comprehensive role of schools is too complex to be met perfectly and often brings undue criticism upon the schools. It is clear that schools need more support from different sectors of society before they can achieve anything near the desired results. However, this assistance must be of a constructive nature, in contrast to measures advocated in some quarters. There are those, for example, who would have schools become more product-oriented and function as an assembly line, labeling students as successes or rejects.

Concern about this was expressed by Elkind (1981) when he said:

> Schools today hurry children because administrators are under stress to produce better products. This blinds them to what we know about children and leads them to treat children like empty bottles on an assembly line getting a little fuller each grade level. When the bottles don't get full enough, management puts pressure on the operator (the teacher), who is now held accountable for filling his or her share of the bottles and on quality control (making sure the information is valid and that the bottle is not defective) (p. 48).

There is a temptation, in view of public pressures, for schools to set standards that not all students can meet. The danger is that this will cause some to fail and become losers in a school system that is not geared to prepare them for life beyond school. Schools must create a system in which any student who has a good attitude and makes a reasonable effort can obtain the knowledge and skills that give him/her a fair chance to fit into society. A "tough" curriculum with high standards may impress voters but at the same time fail to fulfill the traditional school mission of serving everyone's needs.

Schools should avoid the narrowness of elitism if they are to serve all of society, but this is not to say that the very best students should not be highly challenged and prepared to fulfill their full potential for success. It does mean that the critical problems of society, reflected in the high rates of school drop-outs, illiteracy, unemployment, drug use, and crime make it mandatory for schools to continue serving their traditional role of providing educational opportunity for everyone. This opportunity has at least two essential components: an open door policy of education for everyone (which is reasonably well satisfied at present); and school programs and attitudes that are responsive to all.

2. Teachers are under-appreciated and often have to cope with inadequate resources, low salaries, and poor teaching conditions. The complexities of operating a first-rate school system that meets the legitimate demands placed on education require resources beyond those available in most school districts. This often produces the following syndrome: a lack of adequate resources which causes some areas of school performance to suffer, engendering complaints and calls for improvement from parents and communities, who may then make additional demands for schools to remedy ills outside their purview. This creates further disenchantment on both sides and places schools in the position of promising more than their limited resources can deliver, causing stress in teachers and administrators who "burn out" trying to fulfill the many diverse demands upon them.

Both new and experienced teachers often work under conditions and salary scales they consider beneath their dignity. The public response, in some cases, is that some teachers perform so badly they don't deserve the salaries they already receive. Broudy (1985), however, cites a Gallup poll showing that parents of school children consistently rate teachers highly, and offers the following perspective:

In common parlance, school teaching is referred to as a profession. Teachers are expected to have college degrees; they are licensed by the state and belong to professional organizations. Their work requires the combination of theory and skill that distinguishes it both from a craft and from pure scholarship. However, despite the existence of colleges of education and departments of educational studies at many universities for a half century or more, the common reference to teaching as a profession does not reflect the actual status of the classroom teacher as measured by remuneration and social and academic recognition. More indicative of their status is that whenever the nation's schools come under fire—as they are likely to do each decade—invariably the blame falls on the alleged incompetence of the teacher. The complaints take two forms: teachers do not know their subjects; and if perchance they do, they cannot teach. Professors in the academic disciplines place the blame on colleges of education and, more particularly, on education courses. That Gallup polls consistently find that parents of school children rate teachers quite favorably—especially in their own schools—does not seem to impress the critics.

Those closely involved with today's schools recognize and appreciate the monumental effort most teachers make in coping with their daily classroom challenge, especially the *good* teachers who demonstrate an impressive display of energy, social conscience, and professionalism. The time is long past to give these teachers their due, i.e., attractive incentives and career opportunities within the profession.

3. Pedagogical knowledge and skills are crucial for effective teaching. The complaint that "methods" courses weaken the performance of teachers by denying them a "good" liberal arts education is highly suspect. Both areas are critical to success in teaching. Pedagogical performance requires special perceptions, knowledge, and skills that elevate the profession above the level of a craft or the mere application of "common sense" (which is not too common). Much has been learned in the last two decades about effective teaching. The issue is how to capitalize on this knowledge and bring consistency and effectiveness into teacher training.

Another pedagogical criticism is that theory does not relate to practice. The reality is that theory and practice go together, for one without the other destroys both. For instance, on what basis does the effective teacher act? The teacher acts on the basis of student need. Does the student show signs of personal distraction, a lack of prerequisite knowledge and/or motivation? The ability to classify student symptoms enables the teacher to determine what action to take. The student lacking prerequisite knowledge, for example, needs remediation; the student distracted by personal problems may need counseling; and the student lacking motivation may need a different teaching style.

The ability to conceptualize is necessary for diagnosis; diagnosis is required to ascertain why one action is preferable to another. (Imagine the damage done by the incompetent teacher who reprimands a poor student for being "just lazy," when remediation is the answer.) And where does the professional teacher acquire this kind of knowledge? Much of the most basic conceptual knowledge is provided in the pedagogical component of preservice programs of teacher preparation.

When this knowledge is provided vicariously, followed by an opportunity to apply it through simulations and/or classroom experience, the process for developing professional competence has begun.

In an early attempt to identify concepts in interactive teaching, Hudgins (1974) listed 126 concepts, including definitions and indicators appropriate for teachers. Though this list of concepts is not complete, it suggests that classrooms are sufficiently complex to require teachers to have systematic pedagogical instruction so they can interpret and diagnose events, as needed.

Teachers also need to learn how to relate effectively to colleagues, administrators, and members of the community, as well as the teaching profession as a whole. All these areas require additional concepts based on systematic professional knowledge. Chance alone will not expose teachers to the language of the profession or the wide array of concepts they need to understand. Pedagogical and theoretical training on the college level, therefore, is crucial to teacher preparation.

4. School reform must adjust to current and future circumstances. Though much has happened in the development of education that schools can profit from, the notion that schools today should operate as in the "good old days" is a myth. The schools of the past also had their share of criticism, much of it deserved. However, those critiques contributed to school improvement just as today's critics benefit tomorrow's schools by raising issues that provoke analysis.

Today's school reformers would benefit by reviewing a publication, *Public Education Under Criticism* (Scott and Hill 1954). This collection of articles about problems in education over 30 years ago shows how past issues helped stimulate action that contributed to making today's schools more effective.

Many of today's education issues are the same or similar to those of the past concerning sex education, moral values, and religion in the schools, but today's society is more complicated, making the work of schools and other institutions more difficult. The enormity of the task makes it clear that educators and leaders must make wise use of the accumulated pedagogical and technical knowledge at their disposal in coping with the critical issues facing society and its schools today.

# References

Many of the following references—identified with an ED number—have been abstracted and are in the ERIC data base. The documents (citations with an ED number) are available on microfiche in ERIC microfiche collections at over 700 locations. Documents can also be ordered through the ERIC Document Reproduction Service. Call (800) 227-3742 for price and order information. For a list of ERIC collections in your area, or for information on submitting documents to ERIC, contact the ERIC Clearinghouse on Teacher Education, One Dupont Circle, NW, Suite 610, Washington, DC 20036; (202) 293-2450.

Adler, M. 1982. *The paedia proposal: An educational manifesto*. New York: Macmillan.

American Council of Life Insurance. 1983. *Functional literacy and the workplace*. Proceedings of a National Invitational Conference, May 6. Washington, D.C.: American Council of Life Insurance. ED 235384.

*A nation prepared: Teachers for the 21st century*. 1986. The report of the Task Force on Teaching as a Profession. New York: Carnegie Forum on Education and the Economy. ED 268120.

"ASU develops good programs with company." *Arizona Republic,* Phoenix, Arizona. Sept. 21, 1986, p. F-1, 9.

Association for Supervision and Curriculum Development. 1962. *Perceiving, behaving, becoming*. Yearbook. Washington D.C.: ASCD.

Association of Teacher Educators. 1986. *Visions of reform: Implications for the education profession*. The Report of the ATE Blue Ribbon Task Force. Reston, Va.: ATE. ED 274663.

"AU given $1 million to help future teachers fight drugs." *Arizona Republic,* Phoenix, Arizona. Oct. 15, 1986, p. B-1.

Beers, C. 1908. *A mind that found itself*. Garden City, N.Y.: Doubleday.

Berliner, D.C. 1987. A laboratory science component for teacher education programs. Paper presented at Association of Teacher Educators Annual Meeting, Houston, Texas.

Bestor, A. 1953. *Educational wastelands*. New York: Alfred A. Knopf.

Bestor, A. 1956. *Restoration of learning*. New York: Alfred A. Knopf.

Booming corporate education efforts rival college programs, study says. *New York Times*. January 28, 1985, p. 1, 14.

Boyer, E.L. 1983. *High school: A report on secondary education in America*. The Carnegie Foundation for the Advancement of Teaching. Cambridge: Harper and Row.

Broudy, H.S. 1985. The case for case studies in teacher education. Bloomington, Ind.: Indiana University, Coalition of Teacher Education Programs. ED 272500.

Clifford, G.J. 1985. The shifting between schools and nonschool education: A historical account. In *Education in school and nonschool settings*. Eighty-fourth Yearbook of the National Society for the Study of Education. Part I. Ed. by M.D. Fantini and R.L. Sinclair. Chicago: University of Chicago Press.

Conant, J.B. 1963. *The education of American teachers*. New York: McGraw Hill.

Counts, G.S. 1932. *Dare the schools build a new social order?* New York: John Day.

Cremin, L. 1980. Changes in the ecology of education: The school and other educators. In *The future of formal education*. Ed by T. Hussen. Stockholm: Almquest and Wiksel International.

Elkind, D. 1981. *The hurried child*. Reading, Mass.: Addison-Wesley.

Fantini, M. D. 1985. Stages of linking school and nonschool learning environments. In *Education in school and nonschool settings*. Eighty-fourth Yearbook of the National Society for the Study of Education. Part I. Ed. by M.D. Fantini and R.L. Sinclair. Chicago: University of Chicago Press.

Flesch, R. 1955. *Why Johnny can't read—and what you can do about it*. New York: Harper.

Gips, C., and J.L. Burdin. 1983. Parents and teachers as collaborating educators: A training model for emerging times. Paper presented at the National Council of States for Inservice Education, November 18-22, Dallas, Texas. ED 251407.

Glass, R.S. 1984. Partnerships. *American Teacher*. 69 (Nov.):1, 14.

Greer, C. 1976. *The great school legend: A revisionist interpretation of American education*. New York: Penguin Books.

Henry, J.F. 1983. Expectations of the workplace. In *Functional literacy and the workplace*. Washington, D.C.: American Council of Life Insurance.

Hodgkinson, H.L., and C. Benson. 1974. *Implementing the learning society*. San Francisco: Jossey-Bass.

Holmes Group. 1986. *Tomorrow's teachers*. East Lansing, Mich.: Holmes Group, Inc. ED 270454.

Houston, W.R., ed. 1986. *Mirrors of excellence: Reflections for teacher education from training programs in ten corporations and agencies*. Reston, Va.: Association of Teacher Educators. ED 268655.

Hudgins, B. and others. 1974. *A catalog of concepts in the pedagogical domain of teacher education*. Syracuse, N.Y.: Syracuse University.

Johnson, S. 1985. The fourth 'R' is for reform. *New York Times Education Survey*. (April):17.

Koerner, J. 1963. *The miseducation of American teachers.* Boston: Houghton Mifflin.

Lieberman, M. 1986. Privatization and public education. *Phi Delta Kappan* (June): 731, 734.

Masnick, G.S., and M.J. Bane, with N. Baer and others. 1980. *The nation's families: 1960-1990.* Harvard-MIT Report. Boston: Auburn House Publication Co.

Massanari, K. 1978. Changing conditions and perspectives about them. In *Emerging professional roles for teacher educators,* by K. Massanari, W.H. Drummond, and W.R. Houston. Washington, D.C.: American Association of Colleges for Teacher Education and ERIC Clearinghouse on Teacher Education. ED 152683.

National Commission on Excellence in Education. 1983. *A nation at risk: The imperative for educational reform.* Washington, D.C.: U.S. Department of Education.

National Education Association. 1984. *Report of the committee of ten on secondary school studies.* New York: American Book Company.

*NCATE Redesign.* 1985. Washington, D.C.: National Council for Accreditation of Teacher Education.

Passow, A.H. 1985. Combined efforts: Models for nonschool settings for learning. In *Education in school and nonschool settings.* Eighty-fourth Yearbook of the National Society for the Study of Education. Part I. Ed. by M.D. Fantini and R.L. Sinclair. Chicago: University of Chicago Press.

Plisko, V.W., and J.D. Stern, eds. 1985. *The condition of education.* Washington, D.C.: National Center for Education Statistics, U.S. Department of Education. ED 258365.

Pressey, S. 1933. *Psychology and the new education.* New York: Harper & Brothers.

Rice, J. 1892-1893. Articles ran in nine consecutive issues of *The Forum.* (October 1892 through June 1893) vol. 6, no. 10 through vol. 7, no. 6.

Rickover, H.G. 1959. *Education and freedom.* New York: E.P. Dutton.

Riis, J. 1892. *The children of the poor.* New York: The World's Work.

Scott, C.W., and C.M. Hill, eds. 1954. *Public education under criticism.* Englewood Cliffs, N.J.: Prentice-Hall.

Sizer, T. 1985. *Horace's compromise: The dilemma of the American high school.* Boston: Houghton Mifflin.

State to pay Toyota worker for 6 months. *Lexington* (Kentucky) *Herald-Leader.* Sept. 10, 1986, A-1, 16.

*Statistical abstracts of the United States.* 1986. Washington, D.C.: U.S. Department of Commerce.

Sullivan, H.J. 1986. Education-industry partnerships. *School Administrator* 43: 15-16.

Timpane, M. 1986. Business has rediscovered the public schools. *Phi Delta Kappan.* (Feb.): 389.

U.S. Office of Education. 1951. *Life adjustment education for every youth.* Bulletin No. 22. Washington, D.C.: U.S. Government Printing Office.

Warnat, W.I., ed. 1980. Higher education and the organizational response to training. In *Collaboration in adult learning.* Washington, D. C.: American University.

Wirtz, W. 1975. *The boundless resource.* Washington, D.C.: New Republic Books.